Ron,
I ca   oice
asking me when I would write
my book. Well, here it is!
I could hear his voice as
I was writing. God Bless!
Dan

A Dickens of a Life

Daniel N. Walters

DN walters
July 2020

A DEDICATION

A DICKENS OF A LIFE is dedicated to my all-time inspirational teacher, Hilda S. Frame, the many students I taught over the years who helped me become, the State of New Jersey Board of Child Welfare for helping me find a home, Dorothy and William Brown, foster parents who provided security, hope, and lessons for life, Maria Victoria Anna DiGiovanni Walters, my beautiful wife, for daily inspiration for all the years of our lives; and, finally, all the Saints and Poets who influenced me along what has been a remarkable journey.

* *

CONNECTIONS

I'D LIKE TO KNOW MORE ABOUT MY ANCESTRY
SO I MIGHT SHARE THE ORIGIN OF MY NAME,
THE JOURNEYS OF MY ANCESTORS STRUGGLING
AGAINST THE TIDE, REACHING OUT, PERHAPS,
TO THAT FAIR LADY IN THE HARBOR WHOSE
OUTSTRETCHED ARMS AND MOTHERLY WARMTH
CRADLED A GENERATION OF HOPES AND DREAMS.
BUT, ALAS, THE QUESTIONS OF MY ORIGIN
ARE NOT EASILY ANSWERED OR TRACEABLE
SINCE MY BEGINNINGS READ MORE LIKE THOSE
OF A DICKENSIAN CHARACTER FASHIONED IN
FICTION AND FORCED TO SURVIVE THE PITFALLS
OF A FRACTURED FAMILY SEPARATED, UNCERTAIN
ABOUT TOMORROW'S HOPES AND DREAMS.

DANIEL N. WALTERS

*DANIEL, MARGIE, AND VICTOR SOMETIME IN THE 1940'S PRIOR
TO THE TRAIN RIDE FROM BALTIMORE TO ATLANTIC CITY*

A DICKENS OF A LIFE

A MEMOIR

My all-time inspirational teacher would have turned one hundred and thirteen years old this past June. Happy Birthday, Hilda Frame, from someone whose admiration for you is tantamount to the beauty and majesty of a total eclipse of the sun or the moon! I often wonder how my life would have played out had it not been for you and the countless saints and poets who helped lift me up, encouraging me to reach for the stars, or as Maya Angelou would say, "to rise." Like a David Copperfield, Oliver Twist, or Pip from Dickens' **Great Expectations**, my beginnings had a bumpy start, and I am amazed at how far I have traveled in spite of the bumps and pot holes along the way. I have chosen to tell my story, in part, through original pieces of writing composed during my life. Since I will turn one hundred on June 19, 2040, I figured it was time to document my journey, to date, growing up as a foster child and ward of the state under the guardianship of the State of New Jersey Board of Child Welfare, and striving to become somebody.

BALTIMORE

Before I became a ward of the state in the late 1940's, I was living in Baltimore and remember the death of President Roosevelt in 1945; I was four years old and have a hazy memory of standing on a back porch feeling sad. I have tried to adjust the ocular of life's microscope to bring into focus other Baltimore memories. What I remember is sketchy —no clear beginnings or endings, no birthday cakes with candles, no kindergarten, just a collection of fuzzy memories: the music of the Ink Spots, Bing Crosby and the Andrew Sisters singing "**Santa Claus Is Coming to Town**," old-fashioned tinsel on a Christmas tree, snow on the roof outside an upstairs window, my red three-wheeler tricycle which I fell off and cut my hand, wetting the bed and wearing a hole in the mattress, reaching into a basketful of live crabs and getting pinched, being sick in bed with whispers of "pneumonia" in the background, waking up to loud talking when my grandmother, Violet Ireland, had been mugged on the way home from her waitressing job, beautiful purple hydrangea bushes which lined the concrete steps of our house on Fairfax Road, my mother's brothers Nelson and Victor coming home drunk and falling off the concrete steps into the hydrangea bushes, painful boils and someone squeezing them, and, my bold entry into a local grocery store where I picked up an apple, told the cashier to CHARGE IT, and walked out!

I never paid that storekeeper for the apple, and I suspect that it wasn't long after that incident that I left Fairfax Road and Baltimore. I vaguely recall my mother and Nana, my grandmother, talking about a trip we would be taking. The "we" included my sister Margie, four years older than I; my brother Victor, ten months younger than I; our mother Madeline, and me, Daniel.

When the day came to leave Baltimore, there were no tears, good-byes or suitcases. I just remember carrying a piece of palm that someone had given me as we made our way to a train station bound for Atlantic City, New Jersey on what I believe to have been Palm Sunday, March 30, 1947. Although I didn't realize it at the time, the train ride metaphorically transformed my view of the world when a porter gave me a packet of peanut butter crackers wrapped in orange cellophane. Looking through the orange-tinted cellophane, I saw a burst of color, a change in perspective, perhaps foreshadowing what lay ahead for me and my siblings.

Upon arriving in Atlantic City, we walked to a waiting station where I found myself looking up at an unfamiliar tall man who turned out to be my father after whom I was named. I had no recollection of ever having seen him before. I didn't know what was about to happen to us three kids although it became clearer when my new-found father asked my mother if she wanted to go to have a cup of tea. She declined, and at that moment literally walked away and out of our lives, leaving her three children with a stranger in the Playground of the World.

2

PLAYGROUND OF THE WORLD

Our introduction to Atlantic City, dubbed the Playground of the World, was anything but playful. Separated from us, my sister Margie went to live with a family somewhere in the city. My brother Victor and I took up residence in the garage at Casper's Trucking Company where our father worked. I recall no schooling at this time but have a pleasant memory of being taken to a 5&10 Cent Store in Atlantic City where there were beautifully wrapped Easter baskets in colorful cellophane. There was a particular scent in the air of that store somehow connected to the cellophane wrapped baskets, or maybe the smell of chocolate. Every once in awhile I have encountered that scent and am carried back to that day and those beautiful baskets. Perhaps that had something to do with my becoming a chocoholic! I'm not sure of that, but I will always be grateful to the lady who took us to the 5&10 and also bought us clothing. I believe she was Marie Price who I later found out lived in Pleasantville and had known my parents when they lived there with us as very young children. She was obviously one of those caring saints who came along just at the right time although I don't recall seeing her again.

As the days passed, my brother and I played in the garage exploring things, such as a bottle of 7 UP that contained a liquid other than soda. I took a swig and pretended to Victor that it tasted good; he swallowed the liquid and spit it out. I'm still not sure what was in that bottle but remember my brother's surprised look when he tasted it! Left unattended, it was natural for two curious little boys to get into things, like the day someone left a Casper's truck in gear, an open invitation for my brother who managed to rev up the engine. Imagine our surprise that afternoon as the Walters boys went rolling across a busy street crashing into a building. I'm sure the incident made headlines in the **Atlantic City Press**!

At the end of his work day my father left the building, and we found ourselves alone. The garage was our living quarters. I don't recall sheets or blankets; I remember sleeping on boxes on the floor. I remember mice running about and other creepy sounds that I'm sure were magnified by two little boys with rich imaginations as we tried to fall asleep. I now realize that our father was probably looking for a place to board us. I don't know how long we lived in Casper's garage, but before we learned that we would be moving again, something amazing occurred. I wrote about that occurrence for an essay contest sponsored by the **Old Farmer's Almanac** in 2010 for which I was awarded third place in the country and published in the magazine. The topic of the essay was **THE KINDEST THING ANYONE EVER DID FOR ME**. I sub-titled my essay, A Bowlful of Kindness:

> I wish I could thank the man whose act of kindness occurred sixty-five years ago in Atlantic City, New Jersey. I was six years old and had recently arrived from Baltimore with my older sister, Margie, and my younger brother Victor. Our mother had traveled by train to Atlantic City with us and then walked out of our lives, leaving us in our father's care. My sister boarded with a family, and my brother and I spent our days and nights in a garage where father worked as a mechanic. Come the end of the day, father would leave until the next morning. One night as he was about to go, a friend of his, a Black man said, "Let me take your boys home; it's awfully cold tonight." That simple act of caring stayed with me throughout my later years as a foster child and ward of the state. I recall that moment as if it were

yesterday when my brother and I were given a warm
place to sleep and a bowlful of oatmeal with a delicious
cinnamon bun the next morning by a stranger whose
thoughtful act opened my eyes to the meaning of
human kindness.

There would be other such poignant moments in the years ahead but not before an extended period of confusion, unrest and frequent moves from one household to another between 1947 and 1949. I remember wondering if tomorrow would be another moving day. I later found out that my sister was living with the Bonner family on Maryland Avenue. Victor and I were boarded with a family on Massachusetts Avenue. Even though we were living just seven streets apart, we never saw our sister.

Once again, Victor and I found ourselves sleeping on the floor, but this time it was on a mattress in the kitchen. Active during the day, we roamed the neighborhood, played on sand lots and docks, watched fishing boats come in, saw a huge sea turtle on one of the boats one day, and spent some time on the Boardwalk. One night-time Boardwalk incident has stayed with me all these years. Someone gave me money to purchase a container of those delicious potato fries that were served in a paper funnel cup. Running down the Boardwalk to make the purchase, I accidentally dropped the coins which fell through the cracks. Fearful of the consequences, I hurried down to the beach and crawled in the sand under the Boardwalk to see if I could find the money. Talk about looking for a needle in a haystack, I came up empty-handed; I recall getting whacked for my carelessness.

There were other dark nights during this time, such as the plan to have me steal a baby carriage located in the lobby of a building. I don't know who was behind the plan, but I did what I was told; I stole that carriage and ran down the street as fast as I could! It was a time of turmoil and chaos, a lot of drinking and yelling with someone collapsing from time to time and falling down an outdoor staircase at the house where we were living. I remember police arriving and someone giving Victor and me money to go purchase ice cream. The ice cream part of that scenario was the best!

While living on Massachusetts Avenue, I vividly recall a frightening incident when Victor and I were playing near the docks, and he decided to jump into the water. I began yelling, "Mr. Scoopy, Mr. Scoopy, help, help!" Whoever Mr. Scoopy was, he saved my brother from drowning. Thank you, Mr. Scoopy.

Although the sequence is not clear, I remember occasions when my father stopped by the house where we were living to take me with him into neighborhood bars. He carried me on his shoulders where bar patrons made a fuss over me. That memory lingers because of the aromatic smell of a taproom, a scent that I have since encountered upon walking past an open door of a bar or saloon. That scented memory carries me back to my father's shoulders and those little white seals holding tiny red balls hanging from bottles of liquor.

Several months had passed since we left Baltimore, and our stay on Massachusetts Avenue was coming to an end. One day we woke up to find out that we would be moving again. Someone claimed that a gas burner had been turned on in the kitchen. I don't remember smelling any gas, and I'm not sure but I think it may have been a pretext for getting rid of us. I don't recall who came to get us, but the train station this time was a street corner where we stood waiting. WAITING—that reminds me of a song I composed for an original play entitled O.B.E.. In the play, Bartholomew, the lead character is searching for his identity. In the opening scene of the play, we find him in a bus station strumming a guitar while composing the lyrics to a song as he waits.

Bartholomew sings:

> Life is just a game of waiting
> Waiting for the mail delivery
> Hoping something will arrive
> Standing on a corner somewhere
> For that someone who should be there
> I am waiting, watching, shifting with the time
> Sitting on a lonely bench in depots

Seeing people buying looks and times
Or passing life savers to melt away
Heads turn when doors revolve
Turn again and look away
"Excuse me, do you have the time?"
Just to check the day
It is just a game of waiting
Pacing in maternity
Hoping soon it will arrive
Charging knights across a chess board
Planning moves to cheat my landlord
I am waiting, watching
Waiting, waiting, waiting, waiting
Watching, watching, watching, watching,
Shifting with the time

The lyrics of that song partially reflect my personal struggle as a little boy hoping and waiting for his mother's return. Like Bartholomew, I often found myself standing on a corner somewhere, waiting and wondering who I was, where I was going, and when the next move would be.

3

A SEQUENCE OF MOVES
FROM 1947 TO 1948

In November 1947, my sister, brother and I found ourselves together again living in Port Republic, New Jersey with the Strickland family. From what I gather, my father initially paid for us to board there but at some point stopped paying, and his whereabouts were unknown. A complaint of abandonment was filed, and we children were referred to an agency and temporarily placed on a short term basis with the Stricklands. A state welfare agency had officially entered our lives. As of July, 1948, we were wards of the state living in a foster home.

Living in Port Republic had a stabilizing effect. I attended public school there as a second grader. I have absolutely no recollection of any formal schooling before that. The Stricklands were kind to us, and although our stay was short-lived, they provided a positive environment. Recollections during our stay included attending the steepled church on Church Street up on the hill from where we were living, a trip to the Philadelphia Zoo, a huge blizzard in the winter of 1947, sled riding hooked to the back of a car, hunting for tadpoles in a pond near the school, going to see a film starring the Andrew Sisters at the Port Republic Fire Hall, and falling in love with Helen Loveland, my first girlfriend. What fun we had!

Unfortunately, it all came to an end shortly after we children were questioned about a watch that someone had taken apart. That mischievous act may well have been the catalyst to our saying good-bye. I definitely felt sad when I knew we were going to move again. The saddest moment came for me when I was singing "Jesus Loves Me" in church at our last Sunday morning service and began to cry. Some lady from the congregation walked up and handed me a handkerchief. Little did I know what role handkerchiefs would play in my later life; that's for a later chapter. I kept that handkerchief from the church lady for a long time—sentimental, I guess.

The case record showed that our father wanted to take the three of us to live with him, but at the time he had no job or place to live. And so, a Mrs. Elizabeth Coffee, a state child welfare case worker, came to Port Republic to transport us to our new foster homes in Cape May County. Yes, foster homes, for we were to be separated once again; Margie went to live with the Wilson Family somewhere in Cape May, and Victor and I were placed with a family in Cold Springs, also in Cape May County. There we lived on a farm where there were goats; we drank goat milk and fed the chickens and ducks. We also drank home-made root beer. One night someone with a lighted candle peered into Vic's and my bedroom with Halloween masks and scared us to death. I remember talk about a storm coming and going to see a turbulent ocean caused by an approaching tropical storm. That may well have foreshadowed my future fascination with weather and storms.

I didn't go to school in Cape May but remember another dark moment when someone coached me about going into a store to steal items and how to conceal them. I don't know what the items were, but I stole things. Between the baby carriage incident back in Atlantic City and further stealing lessons in Cold Springs, I was on my way to becoming a master thief! Looking back, my training was something like a page out of Dickens' **Oliver Twist** with Fagin teaching his boys how to pick a pocket or two. I don't remember much in the way of family life in Cold Springs, but like those geese that the lady we lived with claimed flew down to the ocean every morning, we found out one day that we, too, would be taking flight once again.

The happy days of Port Republic seemed far away, and Cold Springs had hardly warmed our hearts as we made our journey north to

Hammonton, New Jersey in Atlantic County. Imagine Vic's and my surprise when the state agency case worker came to pick us up; Margie was in
the car, and we were all going to be together again. According to a written
record, the case worker commented that we three children *seemed happy
to be together again, sang hymns they had learned in church, and had
very pleasant voices.* Those pleasant voices would make their mark in the
future, especially Margie's. Our new home in Hammonton was with the
Aichelmann family on First Road. Most often I found it awkward knowing what to call the people we moved in with. The Aichelmanns helped us
make that bridge. We called them Aunt Tress and Uncle Ott.

Aunt Tress cautioned me one day that if I wanted a piece of fruit,
specifically an apple that I was reaching for, I needed to ask for it. Unlike
Baltimore, I couldn't charge it! The Aichelmanns' daughter, Adele, who
lived elsewhere was visiting one time and observed me moving my hands
in response to music. She asked me to repeat the motions again; I did but
didn't know why she wanted me to. Adele's brother David lived next door
to the Aichelmanns and had a son who was born with club feet and wore
casts. Across the street from David lived the Willingmeir girls, Edith and
Lila, whose parents owned a florist shop. Once again I fell in love; they
were very pretty majorettes in the high school band, and I can still see
them practicing baton twirling routines. Down the street from us lived the
Wentzel family who also had foster children living with them with whom
we played. I went to school, third grade, and Ms. Erichetto was my teacher.
At Christmas time, members of a local Moose Club distributed stockings
filled with toys and goodies. All three of us got one of those red mesh stockings. Sometime in the spring of the year I came down with old-fashioned
measles, a really bad case that probably affected my vision. I can remember
looking into a mirror and seeing blotches all over my face.

The most memorable moment at the Aichelmanns occurred sometime in the spring when Margie, Victor and I were at the Rivoli Theatre
in Hammonton watching a Flash Gordon film. Suddenly, out of nowhere
came a voice over a loud speaker requesting that the three of us go to the
rear of the theatre. What a startling moment it was! There in the lobby
was our grandmother, Violet Ireland, who had traveled all the way from

Baltimore to see her grandchildren. She hugged and kissed us. Somewhere in the case records was a notation that she had wanted to take Margie to live with her but could not because she had to work full time. We didn't know about her interest in doing that, but the fact that she reached out to find us spoke volumes. I will never forget her visit. Who could give a hoot about the adventures of Flash Gordon and Ming when you have a grandmother who traveled all those miles with all that love in her heart!

A case record showed that we were doing well in school in February, 1949, although Victor's teacher didn't think that he was learning as quickly as he should. It was noted that he was deeply affected by the instability he had experienced. Unfortunately, a variety of problems led to another separation, and Victor was moved in late February to live with the Wescoat family in Nesco, New Jersey. A few months later, Margie and I found that we, too, were to leave Hammonton. What we didn't know was that we were moving to the same town where Victor was living. I believe it was the same state child welfare case worker, Elizabeth Coffee, who drove us to our new destination where we were introduced to the Browns, William and Dorothy, our new foster parents who lived on Pleasant Mills Road in Nesco, New Jersey. The date was June 13, 1949, perhaps the luckiest thirteenth day of any month in our lives! Hallelujah!

William and Dorothy Brown

4

NEW FAMILY AND A RITE OF PASSAGE

In Thornton Wilder's play, ***Our Town,*** Emily, who has died, is asked to choose one day in her life to return to Grover's Corners. She chose her twelfth birthday. If I were asked that question, I would most likely choose June 13, 1949, the day that Margie and I arrived in Nesco at our new foster home with the Browns. I choose that day because it opened the door to opportunity, stability, security, and hope for the future. Naturally, I didn't realize all of those things immediately, but there was something different about this move, something special about this town and this set of foster parents whom we initially called Aunt Dot and Uncle Bill.

Aunt Dot's sister Hazel, who readily became my favorite aunt, arrived at the house to welcome us the day we arrived. Bill and Dorothy had no children of their own; Aunt Hazel and Uncle Leo Landy had two young children, Leo Jr. and Theresa. Uncle Leo, a natural florist with whom I would have a special relationship in the future, had been in the Army Air Corps in World War 2 where he was a tail gunner on a flying fortress. His plane was shot down on January 5, 1943. Missing in action and wounded, he spent fifteen months in a German prison camp before he was released. On May 6, 1945, he wrote the following letter to his wife:

May 6, 1945

Dearest Hazel,
I am free now. I was taken by the British
May the 2nd. I can't think of much to say honey.

I'll save all the gab till I am back with you which
won't be long I hope.
How's my little red head doing? I can't wait till I
see him as he must be some size, take good care of
him honey.
Well dear say hello to all the folks for me and don't
worry as I'll be with you soon.
How's mom? Tell her we'll have that spree for sure soon.
Hoping you're all okay and healthy.
Yours forever Lots of Love
  Leo

While recovering from his wounds, Uncle Leo was awarded the Army Air Medal for Exceptional Meritorious Service while in action. And on March 7, 1945, Aunt Hazel was presented the Purple Heart for Staff Sergeant Leo Landy for wounds received while in combat over Germany.

Aunt Hazel and Uncle Leo were like a second set of parents to me. My family was expanding. Rounding out that family were Louisa and Tom Craig, the parents of Dorothy, Hazel, Rebecca and Alton. Louisa and Tom Craig became foster grandparents to us kids. The only missing family member was our brother Victor, and lo and behold, when September arrived for us to start school we found him on the playground at the two-room Nesco Grammar School which housed Grades K through 4 in one classroom and Grades 5 through 8 in the other. Margie and I begged our new guardians to allow Victor, who was living about a mile away, to come live with us. Thanks to the Browns and the New Jersey State Board of Child Welfare, Victor arrived in March, 1950, although suffering from malnutrition. At least the three of us were together again, and although we didn't know it, we would remain together with the Browns and our extended family until we grew up, married, and moved away some years down the road. A lot happened between our arrival in Nesco and growing up. I celebrated my ninth birthday on June 19, 1949, and for the first time that I could remember, I blew out the candles on a birthday cake.

Thanks to my fourth grade teacher, Lillian Jewett, I got my first pair of prescription glasses. She observed that I had a problem seeing the blackboard and sent a note home. Off to Atlantic City Aunt Dot and I went to see Dr. Jay Mischler, Ophthalmologist, and Freund Brothers, Guild Opticians where I was fitted with my first pair of glasses at age nine. What a difference eye glasses made! I probably should have worn them long before Saint Lillian Jewett and I struggled together over my learning fractions. Looking back, I believe she was very caring and perceptive, for one day she arranged for me to go into the "big" classroom which at that time housed Grades 5 through 8 taught by that extraordinary teacher mentioned in the introduction to this memoir, Hilda S. Frame. I didn't know why I was going to meet Mrs. Frame, but I found out that Mrs. Jewett wanted her to hear me read aloud. What amazes me when I think back to that Reading Lesson is that I have no recollection whatsoever of being taught to read: no A B C's, no Dick, Jane, or Spot, no phonics-- none of those rudimentary elements. Those eyeglasses not only improved my vision but also, like that orange cellophane that I looked through on the train ride from Baltimore to Atlantic City, opened my eyes to a clarified world that I could now see and explore without squinting. Little did I realize the seeds that were being planted for my future. The Reading Lesson, initiated by Mrs. Jewett, set the stage for a love of literature, language, and words that would have an enormous impact on my future development and educational career. That Reading Lesson was a rite of passage for me, a bridge leading to Mrs. Hilda Frame whom I grew to love as someone who sparked life and interest in learning as only the great teachers know how. She was my teacher for grades five through seven, all taught together in one classroom.

The lessons learned in the Nesco Grammar School (now the Hilda S. Frame School) served me well as I found myself back in the town of Hammonton for my eighth grade instruction. That turned out to be a terrific year! I was selected to be a class speaker at graduation, and much to my surprise, I was given an award at the graduation ceremony for achieving the highest grades in English. Can you imagine that? I didn't know much about awards. I wasn't trying to win an award. I just loved school and learning. Mrs. Leroy Klitch, the President of the Hammonton P.T.A., presented me with a dictionary for my achievement. Over the years, I had made good use of a reddish brown leather-covered dictionary kept in an old mahogany desk drawer at the Browns. How often I would ask about the meaning of a word, and we would look it up. Now I had an additional resource to build upon my growing interest in language, word meanings, and etymology.

My eighth grade English class with Mrs. Gloria Scaffidi was memorable. She, too, took an interest in me; I recall her instilling an interest in the structure of language which I found fascinating. I also credit her with nurturing my growing interest in poetry. I still remember the lines of a poem that I wrote which she had me recite to the class:

Daylight Saving

Daylight Saving Time is here, that's fine,
But don't think you're really going to bed at nine.
Papa says, "Time to go to bed"
What's the use of shaking your head!
Well, I've given up as you can see
Daylight Saving has crept past me.

It wasn't a great poem but a youthful attempt, a stepping stone to more sophisticated creative expression to come in the future.

With my elementary school days coming to a close, I looked back on them with a sense of accomplishment. There were some rough times when I was taunted, called four eyes, and the "state kid"; there were bullies who were either bigger that I was, or just liked picking on somebody for their own egos. I would run into some of that even as I made my way into high school, but my standout accomplishments in eighth grade and my intellect seemed to garner some respect. Back at the Nesco Grammar School, Mrs. Frame was very proud of me for the English award that I had received. I know that I owe the achievement, in large measure, to her influence. I sought to capture the nature of her influence and the impact of her classroom dynamic in a published Letter to the Editor of the **Atlantic City Press** which I wrote shortly after her death on April 17, 1989:

Ex-Student Recalls Mrs. Frame Fondly (May 4, 1989)

I would like to express my personal gratitude and love for
Hilda S. Frame, an exceptional teacher and human being.
I am certain that I also express similar thoughts and fond
recollections for many others in the area who were fortunate
enough to have experienced elementary days at the Hilda
S. Frame School. Ritual, I have come to learn, is an essential part of life. I learned its meaning thirty-five years ago
in the Hilda S. Frame School, a two-roomer located in the
pines of rural Nesco, just outside of Hammonton. It was just
Nesco School when I went there but was renamed for Mrs.
Frame after she retired, having taught for forty-seven years
and having served as the school's principal for forty of those
years. She was a wonderful lady whose passing on April 17,
1989 marked the end of an era for all of us who were privileged enough to have her as our teacher. Teacher she was,
as she led us to autumn leaves to be pressed, identified and
preserved for a lifetime. Lady of tradition she was as she sent
me out with Richard Nelke to chop down our school's tree
for the Christmas season. Primavera she was as she led a
band of excited students into the woods in search of Trailing
Arbutus in the spring of the year. Having woven together a
garland of flowers one spring, we crowned her Queen of the
May. Yes, we loved her, for you see she sparkled and sparked
life and interest in learning as only the great teachers know
how. There was something about that beautiful voice of hers;
it was a musical instrument. With it, she took us down the
Mississippi with Tom Sawyer and Huck Finn. With it, she
taught us how to spell and articulate. With it, she flashed the
silver skates of Hans Brinker and dug up history, both ancient
and American. With it, she led us into a world of books,
questions and answers, and all of the wonders of the universe. That she changed my life is an understatement, for you

see, I too became a teacher, and today I weep a little, for my favorite teacher has passed away. Hilda Frame was, indeed, a teacher ahead of her time. She orchestrated as many as four grades in a single classroom which emerged into an "open" learning environment. Open it was, open to a universe of possibilities where eighth graders mingled with fifth graders, where students were also teachers, where ideas of science, literature and the arts melded together and forged a collection of rich images and never-to-be-forgotten firsts in the hallowed halls of our school and minds. Among those images stands Hilda S. Frame, a teacher's teacher, my most memorable. Sleep, pretty lady. In your memory I offer spring's awakening: Daffodils, Forsythia, Trailing Arbutus, and the anticipated redolence of Purple Lilacs. In your passing I am reminded, again, that ritual is an essential part of life.

In sadness, I whisper, "Sleep pretty lady, sleep."

Hilda S. Frame...1906-1989

5

A TURNING POINT, HOUSE WITH A HISTORY, MUSICAL AND LITERARY AWAKENINGS, ELVIS AND THE BELLS

Like the Stage Manager in Thornton Wilder's play, **Our Town**, I need to take you back in time before Mrs. Frame's death and after it. I recall a turning point one day upon arriving home from grammar school. I asked Aunt Dot if she thought we would be living with her a year from then. I so feared that tomorrow or sometime soon would mark the end of our stay, and we would be moving on again. That may have been the day that Aunt Dot and Uncle Bill became Mother and Father to me, for I was hugged and assured that we would be staying for a long time. A poem I wrote on a June 13th, the anniversary of our arrival at the Browns, expresses the passage of time and adolescent concerns:

> It was this day several years past
> When I came for a visit and repast
> To spend some days as spent before
> With a family to care and nothing more.
> To feed, to clothe and to be schooled
> Were the duties to be desultorily ruled.
> To the "state kid" the stigma so harshly stated
> Whenever he was around outsiders berated.
> But a year after the day of his stay
> He sensed a feeling of a brighter day

Since one year had passed but he had not
He remained with the people he loved a lot.
They'd given him love and dried his tears
And this home has been his for eleven years.

And what a great home it was! The house we lived in had an amazing history. Built in the 1700's, it was an old Colonial structure with fireplaces in several rooms, downstairs and upstairs. At one point in time it had functioned as both a general store and as the local post office (1892). It was originally the Old Union Hotel where stage coach travelers stopped for overnight stays. It was also the historic inn where the reputed Tory outlaw, Joseph Mulliner, who roamed the Jersey Pine Barrens in the late 1700's, was apprehended at a dance one night before he was tried and later hanged in 1781 for his loyalty to England in the Revolutionary War. Those old Colonial wide pine floorboards of the house probably creaked a lot on that dance floor above the old country store where Joe Mulliner danced the night away before he was captured. I remember reading Bram Stoker's **Dracula** late at night in the 1950's and being spooked by the occasional creaking, unsettling sounds of the house. Mrs. Frame had told us about Joe Mulliner and the Old Black Stove that was seen crossing the road at midnight on certain nights near Blacks' Farm, about a mile down the road where the Lamonacas lived when I was growing up. I never saw that stove but would have liked to.

Mrs. Frame's parents, Berta and John Stewart, lived just a few houses down the street from us with their daughter Carolyn who played the organ at the New Columbia Methodist Church which we attended and where I was baptized by Revered Ebel sometime in the early 50's. The good reverend had a hearing problem and, fortunately, did get my name right when he baptized me in the name of the Lord. Bernice Watson wasn't quite so lucky. When he went to baptize her, instead of calling her by her rightful name, he baptized her Ben Schweitzer. I must say that we kids couldn't stop laughing and wondered what would happen to poor Bernice with the name Ben Schweitzer for the rest of her life!

Getting back to Carolyn, she taught me to drive a car although I had some practice driving a Farmall tractor as part of our farm work and 4-H activities. In one of my auto driving practice sessions, I almost took out a section of a white picket fence running along River Road in Green Bank. I turned out to be a fairly decent driver although one late afternoon I managed to lose control of Father Brown's Chevy truck in soft sand driving on Moore's Avenue with Teeny Bell in the truck. Nobody was hurt, and I ran to the Lamonaca farm where they calmed me down and contacted my parents. Teeny and her sisters never let me forget that accident!

When I graduated from Hammonton High School in 1958, I was awarded the Anthony Esposito Award for Literature which included a plaque with a quotation from Thomas Carlyle that read: "Literature is the thought of thinking souls." This was an exciting time, for Carolyn Stewart gave me a set of the Harvard Classics as a graduation gift. What a perfect gift! Just imagine a collection of the world's greatest literature for me, a "thinking soul." Carolyn's gift further augmented a rich collection of books that Father Brown had inherited from the Parkers, Aunt Margaret and Uncle Morris, who lived in Atlantic City before their deaths in the 50's. When that collection of books arrived, I was beyond the beyond exploring Richard Haliburton's **Royal Road to Romance**, Rudyard Kipling's **The Light That Failed**, and Hervey Allen's **Anthony Adverse**. Fascinated with weather, and snow, in particular, I fell asleep one night in the bathtub reading one of the books from the Parkers; it was John Greenleaf Whittier's **Snowbound**. To say the least, I awoke a bit chilled! Both the Harvard Classics collection and the Parkers' vast library helped foster my love for reading as I internalized Thomas Carlyle's "Literature is the thought of thinking souls." Carolyn Stewart and Aunt Margaret and Uncle Morris were three more saints whose influence I will never forget.

Our little town was originally called New Columbia; it became Nesco in 1897 although the church continues to this day as the New Columbia United Methodist Church. Those Methodists sure could sing, and that's where Mother Brown took us for church services and Sunday school. Mother had a very high-pitched soprano voice, and I can still hear her singing, "When the roll is called up yonder I'll be there."

Her voice rose high above the rest of the choir's when they all clung to "The Old Rugged Cross." All those powerful Methodist voices really let the Lord know that they meant business. My wife Maria, whom I married in 1964, described the Browns as God-fearing people who gave us kids love, stability, religion, and a future.

Margie and I also sang in the choir, and occasionally soloed, particularly at Christmas time. She sang a beautiful rendition of "O Holy Night." Interesting that she was intensely inspired by Elvis Presley who at one time had been a gospel singer. Her interest in Elvis's "Blue Suede Shoes" and the revolution that he initiated in 1956, the year that she graduated from Hammonton High School, launched her career as an Elvis impersonator. In the 1970's through 2014 she performed as Elvis with her guitar at many family and public functions. She even won recognition as an Elvis contestant at the Tropicana Hotel and Casino in the 90's in Atlantic City where she was the only female Elvis impersonator. Margie's musical talents were special gifts as she had taught herself to play the guitar and later learned to play the trumpet which she played in the Hammonton High School Marching Band. She had a great love for music and also played drums, the piano, and organ by ear. That great ear, voice, and Elvis regalia made her a real star in the family! In my catalog of special memories I can still hear Margie, Mother Brown, and me singing Elvis's remake of the 1927 song, "Are You Lonesome Tonight?" Ironically, 1927 was the year Mother Brown graduated from high school.

My musical ability was awakened one summer's day in the 1950's in the parlor where Mother Brown was playing the piano which she also played at church, on occasion. That particular summer day she was playing the song "Some Day" from sheet music. After she finished playing, I sat down on the piano bench and with my right hand miraculously found the keys and notes for the melody of the song, "Some Day," that she had just played. Just imagine, if I had not moved to Nesco, if I had not been placed with the Browns, if I had not been sitting in the parlor on that particular summer's day, if Mother Brown had not been playing the piano, and if I had not heard the music and used my ear and right hand to play the melody of a song I had never heard before, I might never have known that I could play the piano by ear. With that realization, a magical door opened, and in time I was playing and composing, by ear, all kinds of music. I never learned to read music except for the bass clef when I was trained to play the baritone horn in eighth grade; I subsequently played the baritone horn in high school and later, the tuba. I weighed about 105 pounds back then, so you can imagine that big brass tuba wrapped around me and me around it umpah pahing as I strutted down the Atlantic City Boardwalk in the Miss America Pageant Parade dressed in my blue and white Hammonton High School Marching Band uniform with white buck shoes! I must have been a hit!

My brother Victor wasn't so interested in singing or music; he loved sports and hunting and brought home a variety of seasonal kill, rabbits and venison. All three of us were active in 4-H, and one year Margie won a Hampshire pig at the Atlantic County 4-H Fair. We named the pig Petunia, kept her in a pen, and groomed her until she was ready to be exhibited at the 4-H Fair where she was awarded a blue ribbon. We loved that old sow and even rode her inside the electric fence that Father had constructed. Once she was fat enough, Father Brown and Grandpa Tucker slaughtered poor Petunia, and we ate roast pork, bacon, and a special concoction called Blood Pudding which I really could not stomach!

Petunia reminded me of the field corn that we raised to feed our pig and Mary Bell's chickens . Mary Bell rented the Brookfield House on weekends with her husband Charley and their children Martha, Franny, and Teeny (Charlene). The Brookfield House was owned by and adjacent to my foster parents' home. I recall Mary Bell chopping off the head of a chicken once and watched in amazement as that chicken danced around without its head until it was ready to collapse! I had never seen a chicken without its head dance like that!

The Brookfield House was an Eighteenth Century home that had never really been updated. It had an ancient hand pump in the kitchen but no well water. The Bells carried buckets of water from our house to theirs, and in the summer filled a galvanized tub to take a bath next to the wooden outhouse out back. I often helped Franny, who actually was born on <u>the</u> Pearl Harbor Day, carry those heavy buckets of water. She was my latest crush although she was in love with LeRoy back in Morristown where the Bells had their permanent home. Brookfield had winding stair-cases much like the one leading to the dance floor where Joe Mulliner was captured in our house. One day Franny decided that we would paint one of the Brookfield bedrooms. I don't recall the color of the paint but remember my spattered eyeglass lenses from the spray paint gun we used.

The Brookfield House really came to life on the weekends when we climbed a tree to dump the bucket of blood for a play we had written enti-tled Blood in the Bucket! We had that old Brookfield House rocking as we listened and danced to the Everly Brothers, Pat Boone, Elvis Presley and others on the Bell girls' 45 record player. We had such fun as kids running through cornfields, cutting asparagas, picking strawberries, raspberries, blueberries, wild blackberries, and camping out overnight in the pigpen! How we laughed and played and found fun without spending a dime! Teeny Bell was the baby of the family until Sally came along in February, 1954. The Bells actually rented the Brookfield House for eighteen years, from 1944 to 1962. In June of 1962, they moved to Moores Avenue, a couple of houses down from my Aunt Hazel and Uncle Leo. I can still hear Mary Bell yelling at her girls for being boy crazy, or referring to someone as being a God damn fool! She was a great lady. She died in January, 2010. Although the Brookfield House is no longer standing, it will remain forever in the minds of us kids who were lucky enough to experience its history, the old outhouse, Blood in the Bucket, and the tintinabulation of the Bells!

Danny, Franny and Teeny Bell, and my brother
Victor with our dog, Ruffian

Our other next door neighbor was the LoSasso family. Margie fell in love with their son Joe and married him right after her high school gradu-ation in 1956. On May 9, 1957, she gave birth to a bouncing baby girl who changed all of our lives. Margie named her Dorothy after Mother Brown, and all of us had a hand in raising Dottie. I remember pretending to be an elephant carrying Dottie on my shoulders through snowdrifts after a monster snowstorm. I recall a wonderful summer's day running through fields with her in one arm and a butterfly net in the other searching for Monarchs. I remember another time when my wife Maria helped dress her for a special dress-up occasion, and on another occasion helped sew badges on her girl scout uniform. And, of course, Aunt Maria was there to help with Dottie's wedding arrangements, preparing baskets of wild flowers and hats for the bridesmaids trimmed with ribbon and wildflowers. Dottie wore Maria's bridal veil from our 1964 wedding, and in 1968 she was the inspiration, in part, for a personal narrative entitled **ALL SAINTS BE PRAISED** which I wrote and had published that same year. That piece of writing is the heart of the next chapter. I invite you to join me for a Halloween journey that I made fifty years ago to see what I discovered about the little town of Nesco and its people on the Eve of All Saints' Day.

6

ALL SAINTS BE PRAISED

Something special looms about Nesco, a little Pine Barren town in Southern New Jersey. There I grew up and attended the two-room school where I learned about Joe Mulliner, a Tory refugee outlaw. I lived in the Old Union Hotel, a Colonial structure shuttered behind two ancient buttonwood trees; and in school I was special because Joe Mulliner, reputedly, had been captured at the Old Union in 1781. Joe was hanged in Sweetwater for his outlawing, and anybody interested can visit his grave at High Bank—that's history. But, like Joe, I too left Nesco—not so notoriously, I might add—but captured I was by something neither Colonial nor legendary. What it was I returned to find last October on the Eve of All Saints.

Autumn's Halloween magic had always been a charm in the pines. Boyhood memories flashed the spell of the past when my niece's letter, begging me to come to Nesco for "trick or treat" night, arrived a month before All Saints' Eve. She long-distanced urgent phone calls to remind me of our masquerade once I had agreed. Costumes were whimsically left to my imagination. When the thirty-first halloweened in, I awoke spirited but secretive about the night's adventure because some of my high school students lived in Nesco—what a ribbing this teacher might expect! Still costumeless on the "at last arrived day," I rummaged wildly through the school's costume bin. Alex in Wonderland traveled through centuries of drama tossing aside *Little Mary Sunshine*, the *Mad Woman of Chaillot*, *Caesar and Cleopatra*, Saint Joan, Fancourt Babberly, and Donna Lucia D'Alvadorez, "Charley's aunt from Brazil where the nuts come from."

I discarded all and kidnapped Pierrot and Pierette, the legendary clown duet, for their sentimentality and charm.

The fourteen mile drive to Nesco sliced my age in half—one year per mile. Family feelings stirred as I drove into my parents' yard. My guardians, in reality, they had raised me as their son and were now raising Dottie, my niece. Searching the dark and distant fields, as I walked toward the house, I thought of my love for my foster parents, remembering strawberries in spring, sweet corn and yellow beans in summer, and field corn stalks and pumpkins in late fall.

"Uncle Danny, Uncle Danny"—Dottie's cry interrupted as the storm door sprang open. Together again as a family we embraced before sitting down to hot dogs, mashed potatoes, sauerkraut, bread and butter, Johnny Cake, and tea—a real country meal. Between mouthfuls, Mother, Dad and I played "Remember When"; nineteen summers had come and gone since three state wards had come to live in the pines. My brother, sister and I had gone to school, grown up, married, and moved away. Tonight I was fourteen again and ready when Dottie, a patient but restless ten year old, curtly cut our "tea and sympathy" with, "Uncle Danny, where's my costume?" I beamed, pushing my chair away from the table, closed Dottie's eyes and led her into the parlor where the kidnapped Pierrot and Pierette tumbled from the bag I had hidden them in. Dottie's gasp and blue eyes flashed the magic I had woven, and she disappeared upstairs to become Pierette. A few minutes later, poor little Pierette returned weeping—the costume didn't fit. I dried her tears, reassuring that Pierrot would not fail her. I decreed that she would become Pierrot's prince and together we would search for Pierette. Somehow she was enchanted by the idea as I almost magically wove a princely costume, draping and pinning fabric, pageboying hair, clasping jewels, and hanging medallions. Dad watched as Mother assisted, a lady-in-waiting just as she had been on so many Halloweens when my wild imagination fashioned costumes for my brother, sister and me. My prince crowned, I dressed as Pierrot, and the two of us left to search for Pierette in the Kingdom of the Pines.

Moonlight exposed walking shadows and smoky breath of witches, devils, monsters and dragons out for their treats. My niece giggled and stage-whispered the names of those whom she recognized from her sixth grade class. I regretted that I wouldn't have known them, even if they had removed their masks; and then I thought—perhaps foolishly—that my friends from Halloweens Past might be tonight's mysterious masqueraders. I remembered a line that someone said I should use in a play sometime: **And then we grew up.** It was that "growing up" here in Nesco that was so clear to me tonight. All that is Wilder's **Our Town** goes on here.

The "Our Town" folks welcomed us warmly. At the Johnsons, my psychic powers were realized when Linda, one of my students, whispered in my ear, "This should be worth an A, don't you think?"—a prophecy come true and I hadn't even removed my mask! Linda, now a senior in my English class, had recently written about a memory in a composition. In it she recalled my piano playing and hymn singing at Nesco's New Columbia Methodist Church—"When the roll is called up yonder, I'll be there."

Tonight's roll call had to include another very special house beyond Wescoat Street on the back avenue. There live my adopted relatives: Aunt Hazel, Uncle Leo, and Grandmother Irish Wit. Grandmother Craig, who is eighty-three, naturally recognized me in spite of my mask; but it didn't matter, for she is Pierette whose magic is ageless. Looking at her, I thought of Grandpa Tucker, her husband, gone now. I remembered picking raspberries for them in summer, basketing sweet potatoes in the fall, and gorging sickle pears from the tree at the old homestead until my stomach ached forever. Many Halloweens were spiced with treats from adopted relatives.

Dottie and I masqueraded on to the Bells' house down the street from grandmother. They used to come to Nesco on weekends from Morristown, and then their kids grew up, moved away, and married. Mary and Charley, mother and father Bell, settled here. As kids we often joked about their name, and I felt a lump inside when Mrs. Bell said, "I just thought you'd be around tonight." Her story of the candle-lighted pumpkin, taped together on the front porch after thieves in the night had run off with it and smashed it in Abbott's field, brought back memories of Franny, Teeny, and Martha

Bell, blueberry picking, and leftover conversations at the Bells. As Pierrot and Prince left the Bells, that taped up pumpkin on the stoop somehow lighted a vision: people like Mary Bell had thought me important enough years ago to be held together. It really was All Saints' Eve.

The saints, however, couldn't dispel the night's chill, and Dottie's shivers pointed us homeward after a few more stops. The warmth of the Wares, Damingers and Fairmans was a temporary and pleasant escape from the outside. Mrs. Ware, who made the best peanut butter cookies in the world at the two-room when I was in grade school, wept a little as Pierrot removed his mask. The Damingers' daughter Jill, one of my students, laughed when she discovered me disguised. And the Fairmans—well, I helped them fill out a "complicated form" while we reminisced about everyday wonderful things—like yesterdays.

After leaving Dottie at the Old Union, I drove down the street for one last special treat. The Lamonacas, too, for some reason, had expected me tonight as they pulled me into their always warm kitchen where we crowded around coffee, pie, and "Let's Talk." They told me that my coming was like having their Donald or Charley back home. We drank to that, and although my visit was short, it carried with it both love and respect; for they had taught me years ago the meaning of tolerance and understanding at a time when the world seemed so teenage tough.

Autumn's Halloween magic was falling asleep in the pines as I stopped by the Old Union to say good-night to my parents. Dottie kissed me a "thank you" for coming. Driving away, still costumed, I laughed at the thought of anyone seeing a clown driving a car. An endless unlighted roadway carried me from the Old Union Inn where a Revolutionary War spy and a happy boy had been caught so many years ago. Perhaps tonight on All Hallows' Eve someone will see the old tin stove crossing the road near Blacks' farm. Or, maybe the Jersey Devil might just make an appearance. Who can say? All that history and legend haunt Nesco still, but the town's specialty isn't Colonial or legendary. It is, rather, the fruit and beauty of the earth, a country meal, parent-guardians, adopted relatives, the love of a niece and the creation of a costume, my students, hymn sings, Mary Bell's taped-up pumpkin, Mrs. Ware's peanut butter cookies and tears, and the Lamonacas' tolerance and understanding—what a collection of Pierettes! ALL SAINTS BE PRAISED!

_The Old Union Hotel

7

HIGH SCHOOL AND COLLEGE RECOLLECTIONS

I take pride in being a life-long learner. My love for learning, instilled by Hilda Frame and nurtured by high school teachers after her, set the stage for my continued pursuit of knowledge. In Hammonton High School I excelled and as mentioned earlier was awarded the Anthony Esposito Literature Award at graduation with a plaque that read, "Literature is the thought of thinking souls" (Thomas Carlyle). I was also inducted into the National Honor Society as a junior and graduated in a tie for third place in the graduating class on my birthday, June 19, 1958. That Carlyle quotation really stirred my imagination and was a catalyst, in part, for the direction of my college education and future career. I would be remiss in not mentioning several high school teachers who were highly instrumental in my development and achievements: Marjorie Peeples, English 1, John Murphy, English 2 and Latin 1 and 2, Mildred Falciani, English 3, Jacqueline Park, English 4, John Reismiller, World History, Harold Yehl, Biology, Neil Pastore, Chemistry, and Lynn Blecker, Band and Vocal Music. I salute all of them as additional "saints" who helped me grow intellectually and emotionally.

I knew upon graduation from high school that I wanted to be an English teacher. I had applied and was accepted to Glassboro State Teachers College where I matriculated in September, 1958. Glassboro State College, which is now Rowan University, awarded me a tuition scholarship and proved to be a rich learning environment. Having passed an entrance exam, I was exempt from taking a freshman English course and permitted to elect another course in its place. I chose Creative Writing where I met a memorable folklore professor, Dr. Marie Campbell, whose rich background and publishing experience lit my fire! While at Glassboro, she offered me her theatre tickets to the Academy of Music in Philadelphia where I attended a Van Cliburn performance, shortly after he had won the first ever International Tchaikovsky Piano Competition.

Other instructors and literary studies profoundly influenced my love for literature, learning, critical thinking, and teaching style. Courses in Shakespeare, American Literature, Classical Literature, Romanticism, World Drama, Advanced Writing, and Literary Seminars sparked my imagination, intellect, and growing knowledge. My Junior Practicum and Senior Student Teaching experiences enabled me to apply both skills and content learned through the extraordinary tutelage of Dr. Mary Bradbury, Dr. Nathan Carb, Dr. John Roch, Professor Leilia Villa, Professor David Lloyd, Professor Michael Kelly, Dr. Vivian Zinken, Dr. Harold Wilson, and Dr. James McKenzie.

At Glassboro, I sang and toured with the concert choir under the direction of Clarence Miller. In a microbiology course I performed an experiment that led to my successfully isolating a nitrogen-fixing bacteria, Azotobacter. I worked as a lab assistant for a Dr, Hussein, my Botany professor, where I applied some of the knowledge and expanded the skills I had learned in high school with my biology teacher, Mr. Harold Yehl, and my chemistry teacher, Mr. Neil Pastore.

Charley Rieckman, one of my best friends, and I had a zoology class together which led to an unforgettable moment when the professor was explaining the result achieved upon crossing a horse and a donkey. I turned to Charley and said, "Did he say the result is a MUTE?" The two of us cracked up and will never forget that MULISH moment! We laughed forever!

I had many good friends at Glassboro, mainly Section 10 English majors, roommates: Mike Weislow, Doug Johnson, Bill Patterson, Charley Johnson, Dick Smith and Bob Staats; special friends: Terry Ballero, Claire

Black, Larry Lucas, Tom Wriggins, Karl Wojtech, Rosalie Garofolo, Jimmy Albano, Elna Mae Dilks, and, of course, Charley Rieckman.

A few paragraphs back, I made a reference to my high school English teacher, Mildred Falciani. Well, as fate would have it, in my senior year of college I was reunited with her when she was assigned to be my cooperating teacher during my student teaching semester at Oakcrest Regional High School in Mays Landing, New Jersey. What an amazing semester that was; my passion for teaching was fully realized. I was on my way.

I graduated *cum laude* from Glassboro on June 7, 1962 and was awarded a Bachelor of Arts degree in Secondary English. At graduation I also received the Mildred Maxson Medallion presented to the graduate demonstrating the most promise in the field of English. I was one of twenty-nine graduates recognized among WHO'S Who in American Colleges and Universities. Looking back, I could hardly believe what the "state kid" had accomplished from 1949 to 1962, in just thirteen short years!

While at Glassboro I was honing my writing skills and had three poems published in the 1960 issue of Avant, the college literary magazine.

The "*Poet's Plight*" captures the internal struggle between the writer and exposure of his work:

> To take the time
> To write in rhyme
> A passing thought or lay
> Which comes to mind in some odd way
> Exposes my helpless newly born
> To the whip and lash of public scorn

"*Seduction*" is an experiment in sound employing alliteration:

> Fireflies flicker flirtatiously
> Canines clamor chorally
> Bullfrogs beller boisterously
> Owls ooh ominously
> Mosquitoes munch menacingly

Crickets chirp charmingly-
Sound-seducing Summer

And, *"The Heavens Resound"* depicts a Romantic description of an impending storm:

An eye encompasses a floating mass
Of buffy swirls and threaded glass
Tinged with a delicate virgin white
O'erlapped by bleakness depicting night.
The hazy mass diffuses rays
Casting shadows excluding day's
Light from a vast expanse beneath
Leading to a change crowned by a wreath.
Faint touches of blue disappear;
A heaven of multiple crashes create fear.
A rumble, a flicker, those unnatural calls
From the secret voice of mystical walls.

I recall Dr. Nathan Carb, a professor of Romanticism, telling me that I was one of the only true Romantics that he knew. Oh, yes, I had steeped myself in the world of the great Romantics: Blake, Wordsworth, Coleridge, Byron, Keats and Shelley. And, as I was growing up in the Pine Barrens, Hilda Frame had nurtured a love of nature as we went looking for Trailing Arbutus in the spring. At home on the farm I worked in the fields cultivating a variety of vegetables and picked raspberries, strawberries, and blueberries. I recall with my mind's eye the jewel-laced spider webs created overnight by early morning dew as we made our way into the blueberry fields at seven A.M. I can taste those sweet teaberries gathered while foraging the woods. I can smell those beautiful purple and white lilac blossoms, and the daffodils, and climbing purple wisteria, and sweet Lilies of the Valley announcing Spring! I can hear the haunting, distant sound of the Whippor-Will in summer, reminding me of John Keats' **Ode to A Nightingale**. I remember rolling in autumn leaves of vibrant colors and looking for deep-in-the-forest holly trees with magnificent red berries which I gathered for holiday decorating.

And when I graduated in 1962 from Glassboro, Dr. Carb wrote in my yearbook, "To one of the few Wordsworthian enthusiasts in the game today—there is a spirit in the woods, dammit!" A spirit in the woods—what a beautiful phrase!

The phrase aligns with my poetic sense and my Uncle Leo Landy calling me from atop a tall pine tree somewhere in our distant past when he had me climb that tree to view a wonder of nature. How I loved my Aunt Hazel and Uncle Leo; they called him Nature Boy during his captivity in World War 2. I mentioned earlier in this memoir about a special relationship I had with him which I will cherish forever and managed to capture, in part, in a personal essay I had published entitled "*A SWINGER OF CATTAILS.*" As a kid, you might have smoked punk; that's a cattail! Well, I worked side by side with my Uncle Leo in the 1950's and 1960's cutting cattails in the swampy meadows of the Pine Barrens of South Jersey. At the end of a day's work, we would bundle our "cats" and take them back to the workshop where we began the process of cleaning and curing them to be sold, shipped, and used for dried floral arrangements around the world. I spent approximately five years composing and editing "*A Swinger of Cattails,*" an extraordinary adventure that further captured my Romantic spirit and love for nature.

Climb aboard a row boat and travel with my Uncle Leo and me down the Mullica River, Wading River, or muddy swampland in Marigold in search of Typha latifolia, otherwise known as the common cattail. You are in for a fascinating adventure!

8

A SWINGER OF CATTAILS

I have swung through birches with Robert Frost, through jungles with aspiring Tarzans, through mid-air with daring trapeze artists, and through Jersey swamps to capture beautiful "cats." Of all these experiences, the most real and exciting has been my adventure on Jersey shores in pursuit of the *flora feline* commonly known as Cattail.

My adventure began in the 50's with my Uncle Leo Landy, a natural florist, who collects "cats," bayberry and other indigenous plants which can be cured and dried to last forever. The cattail ranks high in his collection of wild flora, and each year we sickle thousands which, after curing, are sent throughout the world to beautify store window displays and homes after frosts have silenced other plants until spring's return. Unlike marigolds and zinnias, the cattail, once captured, can withstand a thousand weathers.

It is the capturing of these non-carnivorous wildcats that excites me in June and July when the season for hunting them is in. My uncle and I rise early to prepare for our expedition into the marshlands of South Jersey. Aboard his truck we load our gear: sharpened sickles, ropes, boat and oars, insect repellent, lunch bags and a jug of water. We are both aptly dressed in last year's mud-stained pants, shirts and sneakers so that any old meadow friends can readily recognize the hunters. Armed for the adventure, we rise with the sun to roll toward Jersey's rivers and marshes where gnats. mosquitoes, red-winged blackbirds, cut grass, poison ivy, snakes, muskrats and swaying reeds wait to entertain us.

Upon reaching a likely hunting region, we hasten to unload boat and gear, rub down to repel buzzing pests, and oar off for the river's marshes. Excitement mounts with every stroke, and although these cats can't run, a careful eye is needed to sight their tails which are often hidden in hunting grounds somewhat foreign to the common lover or seeker of wildlife. A sudden cessation of our splashing tells me that Uncle Leo has spotted our prey. He says he can spot them a mile away, and I've come to believe him since he is a seasoned cattailer whose adventures began in 1939. Once the area is sighted, we zero in to make the kill. The boat is anchored by looping an oar shoved deep into oily black marsh mud. If the tide is out, an old stump can usually be found to protect our water jug and lunches from the sun and meadow prowlers. The prized game wait in silence as we begin sickling a path leading from the boat to places undiscovered and unknown except for skillful cattailers, or perhaps, Indians and trappers.

My uncle, leading the expedition, displays traits comparable to the unique marsh fauna that slide or dart from nowhere to break the silence when human feet trespass on inhuman soil. Uncle is a sort of Ramar of the Meadows and never invades the muskrat hole; some seventh sense that he possesses bars him from getting snared, although I often find myself trapped in them. It's part of the excitement, however, and allows the mind to create monster muskrats from which one manages to escape. In the course of such unexpected deviations, uncle usually arrives at Cat Country before I do. Safe from the muskrats at last, I stumble courageously along Ramar's trail and reach the promised land where the game is to be found. There they stand rooted and defenseless as Wordsworth's daffodils. Yes, without exaggeration I have seen ten thousand at a glance "swaying their heads in sprightly dance," especially when the wind forced me to cut through it to hook my cats with a swinging sickle. Both Uncle Leo and I slice the reeds with purpose and determination as humidity increases and sweat burns eyes and drenches last year's clothing. Secondary trails are cut, and the captured victims are bundled in thousands to be carried down the main artery to the boat. Insect repellents lose strength as flies and mosquitoes attack bodies weakened by the onslaught of cats, cut grass, and bent backs burdened by thousands of waterlogged reeds. And so, once the cattails have been lugged to the boat after a few more encounters with the monster muskrats, we make our way to the old stump protecting bread and water.

Lunch in the meadows isn't fancy, but there's a wonderful charm to be found; for there it's peaceful, and lying supine with giant reeds, red-winged blackbirds, and blue sky above, one sees the world how he'd like it to be.

Rested and successful, we hunters row back to the truck, unload the sacred cats and journey homeward to strip them of their green leaves and pollen to prepare them for the drying process which will preserve them forever. It should be noted that the cattail is 90% water, and the removal of that water involves a ritual known only to my uncle and me, since all cat-tailers do not dry them as we do. To divulge the secret would be the same as breaking into an ancient tomb with a curse, the punishment worse than the wrath of Pasht, the ancient cat goddess of Egypt. Thus, as the cat became most sacred of animals to the Egyptians, I have come to regard our floral cats and their preservation with reverence and secretiveness.

After the drying phase of the cats is completed, any moldy ones (those that proved too temperamental or high-strung) are discarded; and the successfully dessicated are stripped again of any final "fur" and their stems cut to a specific length on a chopping block. Then, boxed carefully for shipment, these transported "meadow-mewers," greatly reduced in size by loss of moisture, appear as natural, slender, bronzed cigars with twenty-four inch reed filters.

The cattail season passes quickly as thousands of the reeds are gathered before the tiny bumps appear on the cats' heads indicating that everything has its season, and seeding time is near. My uncle and I know the signs, and in the final cutting there is an air of sadness for me because thousands danced and were saved to beautify floral bouquets; but thousands more grew too old and seeded before they could be cut. Hope rises though in the cattailer's heart, for as I lay aside my muddy sneakers and squalid trousers, I look to the sun with my deeply tanned back and chest, closely resembling the bronze natural beauty of the dried cattails. Unlike the vanquished foe, I will lose my tan until early next June when quick eyes and spirits aim for Jersey marshes where ripe cattails wait to be rescued so that they can be smoked as "punk" to keep away mosquitoes or cured to embellish the world.

Yes, I have been a swinger of cattails and have seen and felt a singular magic in the meadows. My adventure, both real and exciting, has lured me away from society's humdrum and hidden me in grasses taller than I as I sought to extend the life of a reed whose fibers, beauty, and habitat have created for me wonderful recollections in tranquillity.

When Uncle Leo died, I felt a deep loss. He had been like a father to me; I gave the following eulogy at his funeral service:

> *"Life is beautiful, Walters!" That's a mighty powerful lesson that my Uncle Leo taught me. He found it in the simplest form, collected it and dried it to last forever. Sometimes he'd stop smack in the middle of one of our swamp forages and yell, "Walters, come over here!" One time it was to get a close-up view of a red-winged blackbird. Another time it was to climb a lonely cedar to take a look at the wind rushing over reeds in the meadows. That time I thought God had called me as I looked up to find uncle looking down from that cedar tree. He could eat poison ivy; I'd always catch it! He could sense the location of a muskrat hole in the swamp; I'd invariably end up in one. He could make you laugh by reminding you that George Washington had been dead for more years than he had been alive. He could make you think by commenting about some observation of life with a profound impact. He accused me once of reciting Shakespeare in the meadows; I accused him of listening! He was the master cattailer, my hero, who loved nature and lived it. He wove a tapestry of memories that are indelible. Rich memories sustain us, and he was the richest of all. I sometimes think of him as an original pioneer who forged new paths with a remarkable yankee wisdom, a love of life, a sense of pride, a respect for hard work, and the spirit of plowing forward to blaze a new trail. He'll have a good story for them in*

Heaven—what a sense of humor! I'll miss it. Heaven will never be the same, and neither will we.

Thanks for the memories, Uncle Leo.

I would guess that the meadows, red-winged blackbirds and all of nature's wonders were a solace to Uncle Leo, having spent fifteen months in a German prison camp. In Chapter 4, I noted that he had written a letter to his wife Hazel that began, "I am free now." Sixteen years later, on August 9, 1961, I received a letter from the State of New Jersey Board of Child Welfare declaring my freedom and independence:

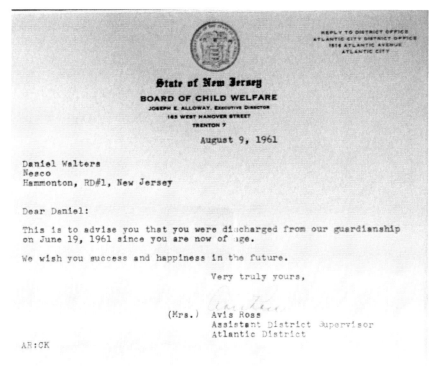

REPLY TO DISTRICT OFFICE
ATLANTIC CITY DISTRICT OFFICE
1816 ATLANTIC AVENUE
ATLANTIC CITY

State of New Jersey
BOARD OF CHILD WELFARE
JOSEPH E. ALLOWAY, Executive Director
145 WEST HANOVER STREET
TRENTON 7

August 9, 1961

Daniel Walters
Nesco
Hammonton, RD#1, New Jersey

Dear Daniel:

This is to advise you that you were discharged from our guardianship on June 19, 1961 since you are now of age.

We wish you success and happiness in the future.

Very truly yours,

(Mrs.) Avis Ross
Assistant District Supervisor
Atlantic District

AR:CK

9

THE BEST AND WORST OF TIMES

That letter, awarding me my independence and wishing me success and happiness, reminds me of John Milton's sonnet, "*Having Arrived at the Age of Twenty-Three,*" in which he expresses concerns about his career, calling time "a subtle thief of youth." Having arrived at the age of twenty-one, I had my heart set on a teaching career which began in September, 1962 at Oakcrest High School in Mays Landing, New Jersey right after my graduation from Glassboro State College and my June nineteenth twenty-second birthday. Sensitive to Milton's view of time as a subtle thief, I wasted no time in launching my career remembering Robert Herrick's poetic message to "gather your rosebuds while ye may." I punctuated many a teaching lesson with a *carpe diem* philosophy!

The 1960's would turn out to be, in Charles Dickens' opening to a *Tale of Two Cities*, "*the best and worst of times.*" The New Jersey Board of Child Welfare had made me a free man as of June, 1961; I graduated from college in 1962; my brother Victor married Phyllis Presti on July 8, 1963; and, I met the love of my life, Maria Victoria Anna DiGiovanni in August of 1963 at a production of *The Fantasticks* directed by her brother Paul Giovanni, a New York actor and director who would be nominated for a Tony Award for his original Broadway play, *The Crucifer of Blood* in 1978.

When Maria and I met, I had just finished my first year of teaching English at Oakcrest, and she had just graduated from Cabrini College in Radnor, Pennsylvania. Ironically, she had accepted an English teaching position at Oakcrest, beginning in September, 1963. I told her on the evening that we met that I would meet her on the opening day of school. Waiting at the front door of the school, I kept my promise, and like the moonlight and magic of *The Fantasticks*, and like Matt and Luisa, the star-struck sweethearts of the play who were in love, Maria and I fell in love. After a ten-month courtship, we were married at St. Michael's Roman Catholic Church in Atlantic City on June 20, 1964. Our reception was held at the Claridge Hotel which featured a pink marble staircase, perfect for the pink and green gowns of the bridesmaids and the beautiful bride dressed in a House of Priscilla wedding gown. We honeymooned in Princeton, New Jersey and at the Chateau Frontenac in Quebec, Canada. These were the best of times.

In the months leading up to our marriage, we had already experienced rumbles of what the worst of the 1960's would bring. President John Kennedy's assassination shocked the nation and the world. I was teaching English that day in a music classroom where one of my students, John Blocker, was delivering a speech, entitled "What It Means To Be An American," when the announcement of Kennedy's death came over the school's intercom. In the ensuing days I saw the first live murder on television when Jack Ruby shot and killed Lee Harvey Oswald, Kennedy's assassin. Innocence was lost as the decade further shattered dreams and hopes with the assassinations of Robert Kennedy and the eloquent Civil Rights leader, Dr. Martin Luther King. For certain, Dickens' "best and worst of the times" description aptly summed up the social unrest, anti-war protests, and the senseless killings of the heroes of our times. Maria and I remember sending young men off to Viet Nam and later weeping for those whom we had taught grammar and Shakespeare but not how to die. Former students John Mercer, Richard Dellarena, and Robert Gasko are among those listed on the Viet Nam Memorial in Washington, D.C..

Resilient and optimistic, determined to build on the best of times, we settled in at Oakcrest High School among a bevy of young teachers: Jerry Hoenes, Jeanette Scoglio, Martin Sharp, Ellen Fagerheim, Bob Walker, Gene Compton, Joe Breidenstine, Trudy Dougherty, Alan Randall, Marge Guenther, Lois Martinelli, Irene Fineberg, Gordon Pieretti, Tony Panarelle, Ruth Osborne, Jim Pope, Beverly Harris, Mel Kerman, John Fineran, Harry

Ackerman, Donna Anderson, David Tobias, Bert Perinchief, Wilhemina Young, Ron Lane, and Hank Kyle. Two of those teachers, good friends of ours, fell in love and inspired a special lyric that I wrote to celebrate them:

IT'S SPRING

How especially lovely is this Springtime
With her brilliant Bud and Hue
Rhyming with almost anything when
Love has joined the crew.
How spring-right to be a Dandelion
Picked and put in a vase
Where she can look in awe as you
Cast Sunshine on her face.
And oh how four-leafed clover he feels
As sweet fortune stirs the wind
To clover-mix with Dandelion
Combining in Perfect Spring.

Yes, love was in the air. Returning to Maria's and my courtship, in January, 1964, I sang her praises in an original birthday card created with pressed flowers which I had gathered many years before.

Happy Birthday, Maria

An aged flowering Spirea
A pressed beauty for Maria
Placed it was one bygone day
In leaves of book in early May.
Cured to bloom when winter set
When earth be cold and not let
Blossoms emerge in wintry season.
Today may lovely Spirea
Petal special beauty in aria
And awaken from her slumbrous sleep
In song with love for Maria

Oakcrest was a great high school, and as young teachers we relished the challenges of teaching in the midst of a rocky society. Our students were the stars and heroes of our daily classroom adventures and extra-curricular activities. I led what might have been the first UFO Club in the country; over thirty students joined the club. Maria and I headed the Oakcrest Drama Club for several years and directed a series of outstanding productions, including **Little Mary Sunshine**, **The Mad Woman of Chaillot**, **Carnival**, and an original musical version of **Charley's Aunt**. Some of the cast members from those shows became life-long friends: Larry Higbee, Diane McGinley, Diane Kemble, and Tom Southard. Maria and I also directed and helped create original senior class night productions for several classes. "For a Star, That's All" was the class night production for the Class of Sigma, 1967. That extraordinary class surprised us by dedicating their yearbook to the two of us. What a thrilling moment! The written dedication in the 1967 Crest reads:

> *One of life's wonderful experiences is to meet people like you. You both have won the love and admiration of all who have met you. Everyone has marveled at the magnetism of your personalities, the magic of your presence. With your talent, wit and warm friendliness you have consistently succeeded in brightening the world around you. It is with sincere pride that we dedicate this, the 1967 CREST to you,*
> *Mr. and Mrs. Daniel Walters.*

The 1960's were coming to a close, and the 1967 yearbook dedication was a significant high point in Maria's and my life. 1967 was also the year that my foster father, Bill Brown, working as an electrician at Glassboro State College, assisted in the sixteen hour setup for the historic Hollybush Summit with President Lyndon Johnson and Russian Premier Alexei Kosygin. I was quite familiar with Hollybush, the residence of Glassboro's President Thomas E. Robinson . Dr Robinson was part of my induction into Sigma Phi Sigma, a Freshmen-Sophomore Honor Society, and Kappa Delta

Pi, an Honorary Society in Education. Both of those honors were bestowed in 1960. I also received letters of congratulations from Dean Robert Bole for achieving Dean's List honors throughout my Glassboro years.

The 1960's had also begun a baby boom for the Walters family, beginning with my brother Victor's and his wife Phyllis's birth to Victor, Jr. on August 19, 1962, and daughter Kim on January 15, 1966. Looking beyond the 1960's, the Walters' family tree continued to grow when our nephew Victor, Jr. married Donna Mazza who gave birth to three great nephews: Victor III on April 12, 1980, Jason on August 30, 1981, and Eric on May 2, 1982. Kim also married and gave birth to three great nieces: Brandi Lynn on July 25, 1985, Lindsay Marie on May 7, 1994, and Sarah Jane on November 4, 2000. Our great-nephew Victor, who also graduated from Rowan University (originally Glassboro State College), married Jennifer Hill and they were blessed with three boys, our great-great nephews: Logan on September 17, 2006, Zachary on March 27, 2009, and Caleb on September 9, 2010. My nephew Victor's son Jason has a daughter Meadow, a great-great-niece, born August 27, 2008, and a son, our great-great nephew, Jason, Jr. born to him and Rochelle on January 31, 2016. Jason's brother Eric and Marnique named their little girl, another great-great-niece, Madalyn, who was born on January 21, 2015.

Kim's daughter, Brandi Lynn, who also graduated from Rowan University, married John Miller, and their daughter Hayden Mae was born on January 4, 2017.

Rounding out this amazing baby boom, our niece Dottie, my sister Margie's daughter, the subject of All Saints Be Praised, gave birth to a son Christopher on April 18, 1981, and a daughter Kathleen (Katie) on August 29, 1986. Katie and her husband Brian Fenlon have three daughters, our great-great-nieces: Kendall, born May 28, 2014, Arden, born March 19, 2016, and Blake Juliet born on August 22, 2018.

Great Uncle Danny and Great Aunt Maria with Great-Great Nephews
Caleb, Logan, and Zachary, Brother Victor Walters' Great Grandchildren

For someone who had arrived in Atlantic City without a suitcase and very little family so many years ago, my family tree has mushroomed! And, I'm not finished yet! In addition to Mother Dorothy Brown, I gained another mother through marriage, Jennie Martino DiGiovanni, an Atlantic City Boardwalk linen merchant about whom I'll have more to say later. Along with Jennie and her son, Paul, my brother-in-law, came a wonderful family of Italians: Jennie's brothers and sisters and their children: Brothers Mike, Walt, Anthony, and Peter Martino. Peter and his wife Marian (Tobasso) had two children: my new-found cousins Peter Jr., and Marianna. I might note that father Pete Martino delivered bread to the Hilda S. Frame School, the two-room school in Nesco where I grew up and where this amazing memoir had its beginnings. Talk about serendipity!

Jennie's sisters were Rose Kelly (children: Sister Theresa F.M.A, and James), Anna Acciavatti (children: Rosalie, Ettore, and Tommy), and Theresa (son, George). And, there was of course, Aunt Millie DiGiovanni, Jennie's sister-in-law, and her daughter Victoria Formica and her husband Dominick with their three children: Charles, Loretta and Harry. Victoria's brother Charles DiGiovanni and his wife Mary also had three children: Larry, Ronnie and Maria. Charles DiGiovanni, cousin to me through marriage, is ninety-six years old as I write this memoir, and he has been a major cheerleader urging me over the years to write a book. Thank you, cousin Charley, for your support!

At this point in my memoir, like the stage manager from *Our Town*, I can see the future and, sadly, most of these adopted relatives whom I grew to love have passed on. You will hear more about some of them in eulogies that I delivered. In tribute to Mother Jennie DiGiovanni and her sisters, I can say that they found their way to my heart through love and to my stomach through their extraordinary cooking! Uncle Pete's wife, Marian, made the best Jeanette Cookies in the world. Aunt Rose Kelly was the Quiche Lady. Aunt Anna Acciavatti made everything larger than life: meatballs, strawberry shortcake, cinnamon buns, and chocolate chip cookies. Aunt Theresa Sanderlin was known for her soups and her amazing Easter pie called Pizza Rustica. And, of course, they all rivaled one another as to who made the best Italian sauce, or is it "gravy"? Well into her eighties, Aunt Millie DiGiovanni, mother to Charley and Victoria, and both an aunt and sister-in-law to my mother-in-law Jennie, will forever be remembered as she arrived at Jennie's door at Christmas to supervise the Making of the Cioffe, an Italian bow-shaped cookie. I can taste them now!

All of those beautiful aunts and my mother-in-law were still alive as Maria and I were completing our sixth and seventh year of teaching at Oakcrest. I had entertained thoughts about further schooling, and during my seventh year of teaching I attended a professional workshop at school which was the catalyst for my decision to pursue graduate studies. I always had an interest in innovative classroom practices and was keenly influenced by the presence and content of a late sixties workshop conducted at Oakcrest by Dr. Dwight Allen, Dean at the University of Massachusetts'

School of Education. Dr. Allen's particular interest was the structuring of time for classroom instruction, and he proposed a model for modifying traditional scheduling through what he termed Flexible Scheduling. His innovative ideas and overview of the centers for instruction and learning at the university convinced me that it was an ideal place for me to pursue graduate work. I immediately set about preparing an application and acquiring recommendations for graduate study at the University of Massachusetts located in Amherst, the home of an all-time favorite poet, Emily Dickinson. I was accepted, and in August of 1969 Maria and I loaded up a u-haul and were off to Amherst.

I end this chapter with a vignette entitled EROSION which I wrote just prior to leaving New Jersey for Massachusetts. It was actually composed on the Chelsea Avenue beach in Atlantic City. EROSION is one of a series of pieces composed to capture the end of summer which I perceive as never ending the same way. It was a topic that I had also assigned my classroom students. I will share several such "summer" endings throughout this memoir.

EROSION

I stepped outside tonight to know the end of summer. An unguarded patrol stand on Chelsea Avenue beach offered a perch for observation of the earlier than usual sunset that clouded chances for an after-dinner swim or walk, except for me and two in the distance who tempted one another with lingering breaths of summer love. Their feet sank impressions where only yesterday the threat of the hurricane forced romance away. It was as though the storm had arrived to sweep away leftovers from summer's crowds, to remind man of nature's powers, and to erode summer into fall. This seasonal erosion chilled the earth until storm winds subsided and fell asleep. I deeply regret the passing of both, but tonight stirs hope as summer's last full moon, autumn's harbinger, rises in the eastern sky forging an ocean roadway shimmering with golden flames ready to ignite the trees offshore and to blaze an exit for

sweethearts, artists, dreamers, and others, like me, who stepped
outside tonight to know the end of summer.

In a sense, leaving Oakcrest High School marked the end of a season. I was certain that I would teach again. Twenty years had passed since I arrived in Nesco as an awkward little boy. Through my foster parents, caring teachers, friends, and adopted relatives I worked my way through the trials of adolescence. Somewhere along the road, I remember looking in a mirror and saying to myself that if I was going to achieve something, it had to be through hard work and my own effort; nobody was going to do it for me. As a teacher, the classroom served as an arena for further maturing as I realized how much I enjoyed instilling knowledge and helping those sometimes troubled students who needed special attention; I had been one of them. And, of course, my dear wife Maria and her mother and all of those newfound relatives provided love, direction, and deepening family ties. Strange, in a way, how Atlantic City kept playing a part in my life. I arrived there by train sometime in the mid 1940's, lived with families for short durations, moved on to foster homes throughout South Jersey; and, then, I met and married a beautiful girl from Atlantic City whose mother was certain she had seen me playing the tuba in a Miss America Parade on the Boardwalk in Atlantic City where I was marching with the Hammonton High School Band sometime in the 1950's.

GRADUATE STUDY AND AMHERST VENTURES

Maria and I purchased a beautiful painting in Greenfield, Massachusetts in the early 1970's. Its content is a reflection of a typical New England landscape. In this instance, the artist captured clump white birch trees and snow-covered rocks with a leafless darkened woods in the background. Forty plus years since that purchase, the painting rests in its original wooden frame above the fireplace in our den. In its simplicity, the painting is a window to the time we spent in Amherst, Massachusetts where I attended graduate school at the University of Massachusetts' School of Education from 1969 to 1972. At the same time, Maria worked at the School of Education, took classes in educational administration, and was awarded a Master's of Education Degree.

As a graduate student I elected to enroll in the newly launched Center for the Study of Aesthetic Education under the direction of Dr. Daniel Jordan. There, I worked side-by-side with a group of educators interested in exploring the role of the arts in education and ways/methods of integrating art elements into existing school curricula. The group included: Polly Abel, Jacques Jimenez, Anne Schumer, Rick Kataoka, Susan Brainerd, and me. Substantive arguments and discussions grew out of our interactions as we wrestled with aesthetic elements and issues and their implications for curriculum development and classroom instruction.

My journey was thrilling as I struggled with philosophical questions such as: What is Beauty? What is an Aesthetic Experience? What are

Aesthetic Elements, and how do they overlap in varied works of art? What is the Creative Process? These and other questions provided a framework for investigation and discovery as I interacted with other members of our center whose diverse backgrounds in the arts included music, drama, fine arts, and dance.

There were numerous professors who contributed enormously to my professional growth at U/Mass. Among them were Dr. Robert Sinclair (Curriculum Theory and Development), Dr. Masha Rudman (Reading/Literature Studies), Dr. Daniel Jordan (Centers for Aesthetic Education and Human Potential), Dr. Roland Wiggins (Music Theory), Juan Cabon (Technology and the Arts), Dr. James Young (Head Start Leadership Development Program), and Dr. David Flight (Educational Administration). Together, this symphony of talented and innovative educators assisted in orchestrating my journey in search of both philosophical and practical applications of the arts in educational settings.

During the 1969-70 period of time I did extensive curriculum work in the study of aesthetics with CSAE (Center for the Study of Aesthetic Education) members and completed a curriculum segment. At the same time, I was completing a two-act musical problem play, O.B.E., referred to in Chapter 1 of this memoir. I actually found someone on campus who worked with me in notating the music that I had written for the play. I also wrote a hilarious poem entitled "The Hong Kong Flu" for which a student from Greenfield Community College created a slide-tape presentation. I prepared scripts for slide materials for MESPU (More Effective Student Personnel Utilization) which focused on differentiated staffing and other educational trends. Through a television and film course, Maria and I created an original script and film about Emily Dickinson which took place at her gravesite in the center of Amherst. My fascination with Emily Dickinson led to extensive research about her, and through Dr. Masha Rudman's course work, I created a curriculum entitled "A Route of Evanescence" which I dedicated to the children of Amherst. Leaving the library one day, I found myself in the midst of a torrential cloudburst which prompted the following poetic outburst.

RAIN

It's raining September fifteenth 1970
Multiply the date times the year
And the product yields but a fraction
Of the raindrops that have fallen on
My years.
Once I played in its puddles
Barefoot unbumbershot
Nonsense no sense but not no feeling.
Cloudburst when I was a decade
Drowned out how it could rain;
Showering in a stall full force
The lever jammed stuck.
Blueberry picking thunderstorms
Chased us from the fields
Washed away the roads
And we got stuck!
Try digging out
Wait for the sun's drying out
Nor'easters, warm tropical storm winds, fine rain
Howling gales driving rains
Patterns of low pressure systems
Heightening the senses
Falling down, down down down
Up bumbershoot now
Running between drops
Still getting wet
Wetter, the wettest I've ever been.
And all these drops have nourished the yesterday me
Into thirty years of
Four-fifths of the world covered as I am
Part earth, part man, part all humanity

Cycling through beautiful rain
Cleansed for the next weather.

The Forecast: Burt Bacharach keeps falling on my head.

And on May 30, 1970, four months before this RAIN event in my life, I had been awarded my Masters in Education after approximately ten months of study, and my professors were urging me to pursue a doctoral degree.

During the 1970-71 academic year, Dr. James Young, who was in charge of the Head Start Leadership Program, observed my potential and invited me to be a teacher consultant for that program. I accepted and worked with teachers from all over the Northeast exploring creative avenues for developing self-growth and creative lessons and content for classroom instruction. During the same year I completed course work for my doctoral degree, along with a comprehensive oral exam which I passed on May 12, 1971. Concomitantly, I functioned as the Theatre Component Director for CSAE (Center for the Study of Aesthetics in Education) and spent a full semester working in a seminar to develop a course for undergraduate education majors. The course, Aesthetic Elements in the Teaching-Learning Process, was implemented during the second semester at which time I taught with a team from our center.

In the summer of 1970, I was selected as the Coordinator of Creative English for Project Broadjump sponsored by the Urban Education Center from the School of Education. That six-week on-campus experience was truly a highlight of my career as I worked with 110 Black and Puerto Rican children, ages ten through fifteen, from Manhattan and Harlem. There were many memorable encounters during the program. One of them came from thirteen year old Hector Ortega whom I offered a piece of orange colored construction paper, and he responded:

ORANGE

Joy, a color that
Most people would like

Friendship, funny things
A color that would
Pop out of nowhere and make you laugh!

There were many stories and poems that grew out of Project Broadjump. Hector's response was a leap for me, reminiscent of that beautiful William Wordsworth lyric, "My Heart Leaps Up." I believe I brought some laughter and hope to the children of Manhattan and Harlem; they, in turn, filled my days with sunshine. At times, I could see myself in those children remembering days without sunshine, recalling my foster parents, teachers, and others along the way lifting me up and helping me find the spark of joy that Hector Ortega discovered through Project Broadjump and a piece of colored construction paper.

11

UNEXPECTED OCCURRENCES

Besides my studies and project work during our stay in Amherst, there were several significant occurrences worth mentioning. First of all, we had company from New Jersey: Maria's mother Jennie traveled by bus for a visit, and we were able to entertain her in a beautiful contemporary home that we were renting. She was a remarkable woman who owned her own linen shop on the Boardwalk in Atlantic City where she sold beautiful table linens and handkerchiefs. She began her business back in 1927 at a time when women were looked down upon as business owners. She had actually worked for a linen house on the Boardwalk before she ventured out on her own with a suitcase of linens which she sold by going from house to house. Far ahead of her time, she was admired for her tenacity, good taste, stamina, and ability to compete in a "man's world" where she could dance circles around most of her competitors! At one point, her Boardwalk shop was on the corner of Atlantic City's famed Convention Hall. And so, Maria and a newfound special friend, Ken Krieger, traveled to Springfield, Massachusetts where Mother Jennie DiGiovanni had arrived by bus for a visit after a five and one-half hour trip. She arrived with the autumnal changes which make New England so special. Maria and I declare that we had never seen such a display of color as we experienced during that first year in Amherst. It was during that first year, also, that Maria's mother had sent a birthday cake by mail. Maria's only disappointment was that the cake was a coconut cream which happened to be my favorite cake; she preferred a rich chocolate cake. To this day, we still laugh about "her" birthday cake.

We didn't laugh at the extremely cold winter that brought us a thirty-two degree below zero temperature, along with mountains of snow. And, of course, Maria's mother heard about the extreme cold we were having, and upon one of our trips home hustled Maria off to purchase a faux fur coat as a defense against New England's Old Man Winter! Mother's visit was too short, but we managed to show her the town and take her up the Mohawk Trail to the mountains where we stopped for a picnic lunch only to have it interrupted by an annoying yellow jacket which sent mother into orbit! She had a very operatic voice!

Our other visitors from New Jersey were Uncle Leo and Aunt Hazel who traveled all the way from Nesco where I had spent many hours in the Landy workshop stripping and drying those cattails that were the basis for my Chapter 8 essay, *A Swinger of Cattails*. We were thrilled to entertain them, and I could just imagine Uncle Leo, the master Cattailer, scoping the woods and fields as they traveled from Southern New Jersey to Amherst. Whenever I traveled with him, he always kept an eye open for coffee grass, fox plumes, bayberry and, of course, salt and fresh water cattails, a major staple in his business. They spent an overnight with us at Puffton Village where we lived the first year in Amherst. Seeing them brought back wonderful memories of two loving adopted relatives who always had room for us in their home and hearts.

Aunt Hazel and Uncle Leo Landy

Life is funny, and my next unexpected occurrence actually was related to *A Swinger of Cattails* for which I received a check in the mail after it was published in 1969. I must say that Maria and I didn't have a lot of money to spend with the cost of graduate school and essential living expenses. That check for my published essay prompted, first, a poem which follows, and then a brief narrative about an encounter with the Secret Service that almost scared Maria to death! First, the poem:

HALLOWEEN

Today I received money in the mail
A check amounting to more than dollars and cents,
First payment ever for an article
Reimbursing words that I had writ.
Emily Dickinson would be beside herself,
A position I now hold.
Yesterday I received a letter
From a friend who had read my words,
In content love for what I'd writ—
A tear in verbal form.
Two possessions now I own
Dear D—begins the one
"Pay to the order of" the other.
 I touched someone's heart
 And I'm rolling in green!
Check's spent—how extravagant!
Letter sent—a monument!

And, now on to how and where we spent that check and the ensuing encounter with the Secret Service. Having traveled beyond Amherst to Northampton, on occasion, Maria and I decided that we would spend the money from my windfall eating at the Northampton Inn. We entered the inn and were quickly seated. As we were reviewing the menu, I happened to notice a couple sitting several tables down from us. Upon closer observation, I recognized them, leaned over and whispered to Maria that

Julie Nixon and David Eisenhower were eating dinner with us. That was a little presumptuous on my part; nonetheless, I was excited by their presence. We knew that she was attending Smith College in Northampton and that David was attending Amherst College. Well, their celebrity was not going to faze me. I told Maria that I was going to go over and introduce myself and share the good news about my having been published. Maria cautioned me about the idea, but I was determined. And so, I got up and made my way to Julie's and David's table. What I did not see, which caused Maria to become very anxious, were the Secret Service men assigned to protect the couple. I spoke freely with Julie and David and told them about my *Swinger of Cattails* article that had been published. They congratulated me, and I returned to my table to find a shaken Maria who shared with me her fears when she observed the Secret Service men reaching their hands into their jacket pockets, obviously ready to shoot me if I had made a false move. How naïve I was although the encounter certainly would have made a great little film clip to go along with the Emily Dickinson film we had made for our television/film class.

One startling final occurrence happened some distance from Amherst. In July, 1971, I heard from my sister Margie that our grandmother, Violet Ireland, had died. Her funeral and burial would be in Baltimore, Maryland. I wrestled with the idea of going, only because so much had happened since Margie, Victor and I had left Baltimore in the mid 1940's with our mother Madeline, Violet's daughter. Madeline had walked out of our lives and had not been heard from again for all these years. I sensed that she would probably attend her own mother's funeral. Maria and I discussed it, and I told her that I felt that I should go to the funeral by myself. I didn't want to involve her in what might turn out to be an unpleasant meeting. I knew deep down why I had to go to the funeral. Back in 1948 when we were living in Hammonton with the Aichelman family, it was my dear Grandmother Violet Ireland who had traveled all that distance from Baltimore to see her grandchildren whom she found at the Rivoli Theatre in Hammonton. And so, I took a bus and train heading back to Baltimore, a town I had little memory of and some apprehension about what I would encounter at my grandmother's funeral. Some of what occurred is a blur, but I remember distinctly standing before my grand-mother's casket and having my sister Margie come up behind me and say, "Danny, here is your mother." What could I say after an absence of more than twenty-five years? Oh, yes, I cried, and I hugged her. Her two broth-ers, Victor and Nelson, after whom my brother Victor and I were named (my middle name is Nelson), offered to drive me to the train station for my return trip to Amherst. I remember them asking me what they could do for me. I really had no answer. I came away from the funeral and realized that my deceased grandmother was the only link to the past that mattered. An even greater realization was that I had no real feeling for my mother Madeline. She had made a decision long ago.

Traveling back to New York where I stayed in my brother-in-law Paul's apartment before returning to Amherst, I thought a lot about what I had just been through. I came to the conclusion that the encounter with my mother Madeline was cathartic, that Bartholomew's waiting in my play was over, and that there were real living people who loved me and would never forsake me: my wife Maria, my sister Marge, my brother Victor, my foster parents, Dorothy and Bill Brown, Jennie DiGiovanni, Paul Giovanni, Aunt Hazel and Uncle Leo, Grandmother Craig, and all of those wonderful aunts and uncles I had gained through marriage, plus all of those nephews and nieces and their children's children, the branches of our family tree.

12

WILLIAMSTOWN INTEGRATED ARTS PROJECT

Having completed my basic course work and comprehensive exam for a doctoral degree, I continued my research and submitted a position paper entitled *The Sensitive Plant*, probing what I hoped would become the focus for a dissertation: defining the primary aim of an aesthetic education. Unexpectedly, George Cross, Principal of the Williamstown Public Schools, spotted me in a curriculum course and offered me the directorship of an arts project that he thought I might be interested in. Following an interview in Williamstown, in the Berkshire region of Western Massachusetts, across the Mohawk Trail, I was hired to direct the planning year for an Integrated Arts Program. Funded by Title III ESEA, the program was a perfect opportunity to apply aspects of my work in aesthetics at the university. Eureka!

Since it was a planning year for the project, I worked closely with three communities: Williamstown, Lanesborough, and North Adams. Beginning in the summer of 1971, I connected with a Williamstown resident, Joy Dewey, a trained dancer and educator. Our work was multi-faceted and included the development of a grant aimed at having the project funded beyond the planning year. Developing the grant demanded extensive research, construction of objective aims, school and community involvement; and, of course, a focus on the "how" to integrate arts into varied subject matter content. In conjunction with the grant development, Joy and I visited receptive schools where we identified classroom teachers and others from the project communities interested in the idea of integration through the arts. Besides the public schools, we held conferences at North Adams State College and Williams College to familiarize and engage staff and undergraduates with the aims of the project. Through these and other community contacts, specialists, and arts councils, a coalition of community resources evolved, including undergraduate students from surrounding colleges placed in the project schools to work toward integrating the arts into varied content areas.

The excitement for me was participating in an evolving project to actualize the content and ideas conceptualized back at the university. The project became a reality through practical interactions with teachers, specialists, and students. Through our work, the potential for resource materials and curriculum development, including instructional units for pilot use emerged. Both Joy and I, along with others from the community, provided workshops and demonstration lessons in classrooms working directly with teachers and students as we searched for ways to enhance a child's aesthetic experience and his/her understanding of the world by using the self as the curriculum content.

Although I would not complete my doctoral dissertation until 1974, the following essay, which grew out of a demonstration lesson that I taught to first graders, became a chapter in my dissertation entitled, THE DAY WE MADE THE SUN.

(13)

THE DAY WE MADE THE SUN

I can still remember those children after all of these years. Remember that thought; I'll come back to those children later. As a graduate student investigating the role of the arts in education, I spent hours at my graduate study carrel at U/Mass reading and deciphering Kant and other thinkers exploring beauty and aesthetic philosophy. My search was thrilling as I gathered notes and images, struggling with seemingly simple ideas that seemed, at times, perplexing. I thought I knew what beauty was. I thought I understood structure and form and the relationship of those elements to the arts. Oddly enough, my search for the aha moment culminated not at my library carrel, or in a seminar for applying aesthetic elements to learning; but rather, in an open classroom setting with a group of first grade children—those children that I promised you I would return to. Let me take you back to that classroom in Massachusetts and The Day We Made the Sun.

The exact day was January 20, 1972, when I was both a doctoral student at U/Mass in Amherst as well as the director for the planning year of the Williamstown Integrated Arts Curriculum Project. One of my many jobs as a director included giving classroom demonstration lessons exploring aesthetic elements, such as rhythm, line, or color. On that memorable day, I was scheduled to give a lesson focusing on color. Thinking about the lesson as I drove the Mohawk Trail from Amherst to Lanesborough, one of the project schools in Williamstown, Massachusetts, I created a simple lyric:

> The sun is yellow, the sky is blue
> I'm thinking of a color, can you?

Besides the lyric, I had prepared a boxful of colorful objects as a catalyst for the color lesson to be used with a group of first graders. The idea for the lesson grew out of the regular teacher's request and a cue from one of the first graders who had called me Mr. Purple in response to a tie I was wearing in a previous sound exploration lesson. When I walked into the classroom that January day, I was greeted with "Mr. Brown, Mr. Orange and Mr. Yellow" in reaction to a floral tie I was wearing. I immediately set down my box of varied colored objects and asked the class to find and name colors that their classmates were wearing; the request prompted a chorus of colors. Sitting on the floor together, I then asked the class to think, "If you could be any color you want to be, what would it be? Keep it inside for a whole minute." And then, I introduced my Mohawk Trail lyric,

> The sun is yellow, the sky is blue
> I'm thinking of a color, can you?

And those color preferences that those little tykes had kept inside for a minute or more were released like a beautiful choral rainbow.

At some point in the midst of this activity, there arose a confusion between gold and silver. I remember thinking to myself that I was wearing a watch band with both gold and silver coloring, but something told me to look for another way to make the distinction. Eureka! The catalyst lay within the color box that contained a twenty-five foot garland of gold tinsel. Neither the classroom teacher nor I were sure who made the transition, but the children took hold of that golden object and began circling with it. Before we knew what had happened, those remarkable children had transformed the golden garland into the SUN!

In both an artistic and poetic sense, the garland experience became an extended metaphor. The children's movement intensified the impact of the experience; it was their original creation and through their actions and words they moved beyond my simple lyric to another level of awareness. Circling as the sun, someone interjected, "The sun stays up" which was sung three times as the children found their own lyrics to color imaginations and movements. Recalling that a new child was a part of the group, I sang aloud,

> Ann, Ann, is new to the class
> She must have a color, alas! alas!

Ann responded that her color was black and through corresponding physical movements kept the energy of the sun alive as she raised the garland saying, "The sun stays up." Pause. "And when down, it's sunset." The entire group took Ann's cue and sank in sunset. Seconds of quiet followed before Will commented, "The sun's coming up now, let's get up and go to school." I don't know the words he used, but periodically Will ran around inside the "sun" singing spontaneous lyrics. I joined in, "Like a merry-go-round, up and down, sun up/sun down/around around/around/around the sun goes/revolving around the world" which prompted three children to enter the center of the sun with the refrain, "We're in the middle of the sun!" From another child, "What does the sun do?" Someone answered, "It shines up the world." And Will re-entered the sun informing us that he was a plant, and "I'm growing because the sun is shining—all the plants are growing." And Joseph, who had been given a prism during the activity, held it up and commented, "How the light turns into a rainbow." That rainbow image sparked another extension as Carol informed the sun-makers that it was snowing outside and proceeded to pick up tiny strands of the golden garland which she threw into the air proclaiming, "It's snowing, it's snowing." The children sang the snow refrain, and from someone came, "The sun is shining on the earth again/the sun is shining on the earth again." Sensing a winding down, I took the lead saying, "As the sun slows down, down, down" (the children responded accordingly), "I want you to close your eyes and hold out your hands. I'm going to give you something you may keep, something very special." From the color box I retrieved tiny orange feathers which the children proceeded to put in their hair and on their clothing; some used a stapler to attach feathers to the "sun." When I asked the class how we should end the day, one of them said, "A sunset." Taking the cue, they took hold of their golden creation and began spinning and then slowly lowering their bodies to the floor in sunset. I broke the silence, "The sun is yellow, the sky is blue/I'm thinking of a color, can you?" And from the center of the sun came a burst of colors!

Little did I know how my work in the Williamstown Integrated Arts Project would impact on my doctoral work at the University of Massachusetts where I was a student in the Center for Aesthetic Education. From one of those extraordinary first graders came a drawing weeks after the sun creation which he entitled, "The Day We Made the Sun." I actually used that title for a chapter of my dissertation. The connection of that day to my growth as an educator and human being is overwhelming. Back at the university we had discussed the concept of an aesthetic experience and the aha moment. My search for discovery and meaning of those ideas truly coalesced on that remarkable January day in the Berkshires of Western Massachusetts where a group of first graders took me by the hand, just as Hilda S. Frame had at the Nesco School many years before, opening my eyes to the possibilities that lie within the universe.

14

A DOOR CLOSES AND
ANOTHER DOOR OPENS

My year's work as director of the planning year for the Williamstown Integrated Arts Project was coming to a close, and I received high praise for the work accomplished. A final task was the completion and submission of the operational proposal for the following year. I was pleased to learn that the proposal was accepted, and the program was funded to continue.

Those first graders had opened my eyes to possibilities in the universe. Ironically, I was being petitioned to return to New Jersey for another possibility, to fill a supervisory position at a new high school in the Greater Egg Harbor Regional High School District where I had taught prior to coming to Amherst. The offer meant a return to family and the opportunity to build a program and a new school.

It was not easy leaving the project. Often I had experienced my own private snowstorm as I traveled to the top of the Mohawk Trail and around the hairpin turn from Amherst to Williamstown. Joy Dewey had been a wonderful assistant in the project giving demonstration lessons and helping to refine the operational grant. Nadine, my personal secretary, was a gem. The teachers and children of the communities and participating schools we served were the heartbeat of the program. I learned so much from them. Prior to my arrival in Amherst, I had worked solely with high school students. Through the Integrated Arts Project, I worked with college students and those amazing first graders who had taught me how to make a "sun."

I had more work to do before leaving Amherst. We had made many friends over the three years, including Morgan Circle neighbors, Lou and Ruthann Morell, school of education personnel and friends: Gretchen, Helene, Betty, Ken Krieger and his buddies Scalc, Rob, Neil and Jerry; they all enriched our lives tremendously even if Ken Krieger did finish eating my lobster at a dinner Maria had prepared during which I managed to cut my hand, which bled profusely, on a lobster claw. Ken finished my lobster meal while I was getting bandaged! There was also Rena Goichberg who notated the music for the lyrics of the play I was writing; she had the role of Emily in the graveyard film that Maria and I had created about Emily Dickinson. We also had the pleasure of meeting and listening to Natalie Cole before she became famous; she was a student at U/Mass and sang in the lounge at the top of the student center. It was in that very center, in an elevator, where I met and shook the hand of the "Greatest," Muhammad Ali himself. To this day, I have never shaken a hand any larger!

Looking back, we knew we would not miss the extraordinary snow depths we had experienced during our first year living at Puffton Village, or the thirty-two degrees below zero temperature that greeted us one wintry morning. Nor would we forget the social unrest that erupted following the May 4, 1970 Kent State Massacre which prompted numerous protests on college campuses, including U/Mass. That unrest resulted in campus demonstrations, confrontations, and an audible barrage of political and fiery dialogue among fired-up students in the local pubs.

Thinking back, I can hear the music of the Beatles, Judy Collins, Simon and Garfunkle, Gilbert Sullivan singing "Alone Again" and Don McLean's classic "American Pie" capturing *the day the music died.* And so, leaving great memories behind we sang:

Bye bye Miss American Pie
Bye bye beautiful Amherst sky
Bye bye snow drifts four feet high
Bye bye Mr. Purple in a colorful tie.
Bye bye Atkins amazing apple pie farm
Bye bye Muhammad with all your charm

Bye bye Natalie Cole a rising star
Bye bye Rena and Emily, poet extraordinaire
Bye bye to the Center for the Study of Aesthetic Education
Bye bye to all of those professors who deserve an ovation!

AND

Hello, New Jersey, and the work that lay ahead as I gathered my books and papers. Having completed extensive research and committee approval for my doctoral dissertation topic, ***The Primary Aim of An Aesthetic Education in An Integrated Curricular Context***, I was prepared for my next adventure.

Before beginning the huge task of writing my dissertation and assuming my new position as an English supervisor in a proposed new high school, I've decided to end this chapter on a light note with an amusing poem I referenced earlier. I composed the poem about a not so amusing topic. Many were adversely affected by the invasion of the Hong Kong Flu. I conceived the piece while traveling to visit friends in Morgantown, West Virginia. As a tongue and cheek creation, the poem grew out of a reaction to the images that played on my imagination in response to news reporting which had a rhythmic cadence that influenced the creation of the poem and its images.

THE HONG KONG FLU
Have you had the Hong Kong Flu yet?
I'll bet You'll get Flu yet
Bet yet Flu yet You'll get
By jet So get set!
They're flying it in—
It's in the air Under the chair
Hiding in hair under
Arm pits and half wits
And in Red China's vacant chair in the U.N.

Have you had the Hong Kong Flu shot?
What? Not yot?
Oh, Velly Velly bad!
Consult your doctor
Or Veter-in-Arian—
Why him?
You remind me of a horse and I'm sure that the effects
Could be cured much better by a doctor who's a Vet—
Sir, Giddy Up!

Better get the Hong Kong flu shot—
What! Not Yot?
Oh, velly velly bad!
Confucius say,
"Man without Flu…………….Shot!"
What? Hurry to your pharmacist
For pills Take them every hour
Like drill Work Aspirin
     Or Bufferin
     Or Excedrin
     Or Cope
Fighting the King of Kongs

Hong Kong
     Hong Kong
          Hong Kong

Better get the Hong Kong Flu shot
Don't wait, your fate is
Shocking
          Rocking

Hong Kong is knocking
Knocking at your door this very sec'—

Cover your face Lift your skirt
Wash your hands Clean that dirt!
Those germs are lurking
Better get working
                AXION!
If you haven't had the Hong Kong Flu yet
I'll bet You'll get Flu yet
                QUICK!
Buckle your seat belt for safety
And fly ORIENT
To cheery China's old
Hong Kong
            Hong Kong
                    Hong Kong

There's no denying
People are dying
Dying on streets
Dying on seats
In buses and taxis
In bedrooms and factories
In Kansas and Maine
In England and Spain
It's the Hong Kong strain
OUCH! The Pain Strain Pain Strain
Rain in Spain
Strain in Pain
The Hong Kong Strain of Flu.

People turning colors,
What fun!
Green and orange and yellow
Complexion.
Symptoms are strange

Temperatures range
From 105 to 110
Warm
    Tepid
        Hot
            Boil
Kong has struck American soil!
I want a shot!
Sorry, you're not
Old enough or chronically ill—
Have you got a chill?
Hurry write your will
Swallow this pill
Go home and lie still
Ill Chill Could Kill
IT'S HONG KONG
    HONG KONG
        HONG KONG
            HONG KONG

THE KING OF KONGS!

*World-wide, many people died during the 1968-69 Hong Kong Flu pandemic. As I write this memoir in 2020, our country and the world are battling Corona Disease (Covid-19), another pandemic. In America, we have over a million cases of the disease, with more than eighty thousand deaths. Because of the pandemic, we have found ourselves quarantined, masked and gloved as we follow guidelines aimed to keep us healthy, maintaining physical distance from neighbors, shoppers, and others in communities throughout the country where restaurants and other businesses remain closed to the public. Simon and Garfunkle's "Sounds of Silence" is here.

15

NOAH'S ARK, GROUNDBREAKING, PUSH BACK THE DESKS

Happily, we didn't get the Hong Kong Flu. As I write this, Maria and I recently had our annual flu shots. No Hong Kong, Swine, Avian, or Asian Flu for us! What was for us was a new venture back home to New Jersey and a return—yes—to Atlantic City where I had roamed as a little boy, where Maria grew up and went to school, and where her mother, Jennie, was still conducting business, since 1927, at Giovanni's Linen Shop on the Atlantic City Boardwalk. Upon our return, we moved to 4 North Montpelier Avenue, the DiGiovanni homestead. Always on the lookout for "my end of summer," I found it one morning on the very street where we were living:

> *This morning at 9 A.M., on Montpelier Avenue in Atlantic City, a stop at a red light allowed me time to look up through the windshield into the heavens where I saw a first in my life. Moving across the sky from what appeared to be northwest toward the southeast was a flock of Canadian geese. Oh sure, I had seen the migrations of northern geese V'ing south before. But today's formation was incomparable. Each bird in the V-formed life chain was silvered by sunlight. For a moment, birds became a string of silver-white lights decorating the sky. Sky wore a necklace of shimmering silver wings. Life took on a natural high from this moment of fleeting beauty. Back on earth, the light turned green, and I*

flashed a right blinker and turned with it. Traffic lights seemed
harsher now in comparison to the intensity and beauty of those
from the north that I had just seen. I wonder if I'll ever see
them again.

Over the next thirteen years, Maria assisted her mother, helping to relocate Giovanni's to Central Square in Linwood, New Jersey. The move came about as the casino industry arrived and forced many businesses to relocate. Mother DiGiovanni continued to work into her eighties, and Maria worked with her as well as establishing her own business, M. Walters, which featured beautiful bed linens and bathroom towels and fixtures. Giovanni's was a family business, and many members of the Martino family (Jennie's maiden name) worked over the years in both the Atlantic City and Linwood locations. Mother DiGiovanni's sisters Anna Acciavatti, Rose Kelly, and Theresa Sanderlin all worked in the original Giovanni's, along with Marianna Martino, a niece. I, too, lent a hand, on occasion, and sold beautiful tablecloths and handkerchiefs. Perhaps you will recall my comment in Chapter 3 when I was living in Port Republic, New Jersey and sang "Jesus Loves Me" at my last Sunday morning service where I began to cry, and some sweet lady handed me a handkerchief. I commented then that handkerchiefs would play a part again in my later life. And so, there I was at both Giovanni's on the Boardwalk and at Central Square selling all kinds of handkerchiefs: embroideries, prints, and initials.

My primary work, of course, was that of an English teacher and a department chairman in what became an amazing tug of war! Yes, I was hired for those positions at Absegami High School which, upon my arrival, had not yet been built. Thus, I found myself once again back at Oakcrest High School where I had begun my teaching career, only to find out that Oakcrest and Absegami would be sharing the same facility for a period of time. Thank goodness that I was born a Gemini which helped, I'm sure, in dealing with the dual school setup.

Let me explain that duality which I had a chance to do as a keynote speaker for a Middle States Evaluation dinner. Bear with me, and you'll get a picture of what it was like having two schools sharing a single building for ten years. In my address, I called it the Days of Noah's Ark. From 1972 to 1982, as part of the Greater Egg Harbor Regional High School District, we were docked together in what seemed like a double-decker ark at the district's Oakcrest site in Mays Landing, New Jersey. All you had to do was to look around; there were practically two of everything imaginable: two principals, two vice-principals, two sets of school colors, two bands, two football teams, two schedules, two sets of teachers and pupils, two sets of guidance counselors, two sets of supervisors, one set of classrooms and hallways, and one set of books—all stuffed into a single ark set adrift with one set of oars waiting for the waters to recede! Somebody once commented that we were meant to do things in twos in this world. Be that as it may, we grew fearful of a cloning effect—tired of twoing it (or towing it). Each school wanted its own identity. Finally, a referendum went before district voters, and approval for construction of Absegami High School passed by just ONE vote! I forgot to mention that each school had its own mascot; Oakcrest's was the Falcons, and Absegami's, the Braves. Well, with that vote of approval, the Absegami Braves took to canoes in search of their own territory. They found it just off Wrangleboro Road in Galloway Township. I was there the day we broke ground. I can still see the groundbreakers: John Falciani, John Finneran, Ron Grunstra, Gordon Pieretti, John Dugan, and Ralph Martin—all those administrative types donned in their Indian headbands digging up the earth in search of something eternal as other interested folk looked on in amazement dreaming of a better day. Looking beyond that groundbreaking into the future, all of those distinguished groundbreakers have passed away except Ron Grunstra who served as principal of Absegami High School until his retirement in 1992.

Looking toward the future, Absegami would one day have a home of its own. However, the ten years leading up to the actual construction of the school plant required extensive planning, and each of us supervisors played a major role in that planning and design. My primary focus was the English and Reading Departments and the school auditorium. In addition to working with architects and school administrators for the proposed new school, I had the additional responsibility of building an English department, supervising the daily needs and performance evaluation of twenty-five teachers, lesson planning and preparations for classes that I taught, and meeting with students referred to me for behavioral issues.

I must say that I loved every aspect of my work as a supervisor and teacher. Building curriculum and courses of study enabled me to employ knowledge and skills that I had acquired through my university training. And to my delight, I was able to develop and teach a course entitled Why Man Creates incorporating aesthetic elements. One of the teachers in my department asked me what I was teaching in that class since a niece of hers was taking the course and raved about it.

I wrote an essay, entitled PUSH BACK THE DESKS, as a response to the teacher and her niece's reaction to the class activity. In that essay, I raised the question: Is it possible to unrivet desks and students and still maintain control, making learning a riveting experience in the other sense of the word? I believe it is possible. I recall vividly an extended lesson I taught in which we were studying James Weldon Johnson's poem, "The Creation." I pushed back the desks but not before a lot of pre-planning had been done. Students had been directed to investigate the contents of the poem and to create sounds and movements to compliment it. The investigation led to students using tape recorders to record sounds which they brought to class to be used to enhance a choral recitation of the poem. Additions and deletions were made. At some point, we pushed back the desks, took off our shoes, and out of chaos emerged human voices, recorded sounds and body movements that blended into what became the creation of the universe through a choral/movement dramatization of Weldon's poem. We soared beyond the classroom, the desks and our four walls. Like those first graders back in Lanesborough, Massachusetts, a group of seniors in my Why Man Creates class created their own "sun."

I was convinced that what I had experienced in that creation of the universe could be applied to other content, other opportunities for pushing back the desks. And, I set out to do just that! Continuing with my concept, I experimented with an elective course I was teaching entitled War and Other Human Conflicts. The first half of the course included a study of Euripides' **The Trojan Women** and Shakespeare's **The Tragedy of**

Macbeth. Study guides, dramatizations, discussions, essay development and film viewings all proved to be sound vehicles for processing the content. Students became fired up over man's inhumanity to man through the study of Euripides' classical anti-war drama. Shakespeare's supernatural play culminated with a sit-down test on the Bard's birthday. We celebrated with cakes for William, baked and decorated by two senior boys. The event ended with a hilarious portrayal of the Porter Scene from *Macbeth* by Gerry Weller, another senior. Euripides and Shakespeare had been digested with vigor and intellectual curiosity. We were ready to push back the desks.

For the final phase of the course, I devised a series of learning packets entitled A Package of Human Conflicts. The packets included Robert Cormier's *The Chocolate War*, Dalton Trumbo's **Johnny Got His Gun,** Erich Remarque's **All Quiet on the Western Front**, Stephen Crane's **The Red Badge of Courage**, and the Hubermans' **War An Anthology**. Each packet contained a total of eight assignments, including synoptic and critical reviews, journal and essay writing, oral presentations, and a non-verbal response to the self-selected learning packet. To my amazement, I became a traveling teacher as students set directions for themselves, working in and out of the classroom. A cluster of students went to the Media Center where they watched a film version of **All Quiet on the Western Front** after they had read the book. That same group requested permission to meet in the art room to discuss ideas for potential non-verbal responses. In a follow-up, I observed one of those students working with clay to create his response. Another group of students reading *The Chocolate War* clustered together on the grass outside the building, reading, journaling, and discussing the novel. In another instance, a student asked, "What do you think about our videotaping a scene from our novel after we write the dialogue?" Another imaginative student told me that she had an idea for a different conclusion to the novel that she was reading. I told her to write it.

The excitement generated through the Human Conflicts activity was contagious, and I learned a great deal about teaching, and learning, and students. Students can help us as teachers to push back the desks. Through sound direction, they can learn and be trusted if we are willing to recognize the value of exposing them to other patterns of instruction through the expanded use of space, personnel, and resources within the teaching-learning environment. I ended my **Push Back the Desks** essay with the following paragraph:

> June will soon be here, and my students will have
> gone. Recollections in tranquillity will occur. One
> will be the contents of the note from Kevin informing
> me that he had taken my desk chair outside in the
> sun to read his novel. He promised to return it after
> the following period because he had checked and knew
> for certain that there was no class scheduled in the room
> for the class period following ours. He had decided to
> use his lunch period to read his novel, **The Chocolate
> War**. My response to Kevin:

KEEP THE CHAIR. I'VE PUSHED BACK MY DESK AND THE OTHERS.
PERHAPS WE WON'T NEED THEM COME SEPTEMBER!

16

COPING WITH LOSS

December 1973 was a heartbreak for our family, for on the very first day of the month my brother Victor died following injuries from a train accident. I recall the day as if it were yesterday: the ride to Kessler Memorial Hospital in Hammonton, the frantic drive via the Atlantic City Expressway to Shore Memorial Hospital where he was to be transferred, the waiting room, the news that he didn't make it, his wife Phyllis breaking down, the drive back to our home in Atlantic City with Phyllis, Maria's phone call letting me know she was waiting for Mother and Father Brown at the hospital, the unbelievably warm temperature on such a chilling day. In age, Victor and I were just ten months apart; he was thirty-two when he died. There would be other eulogies in my future. In sorrow, I tried to capture the loss and impact of my brother's passing in a sonnet.

> My brother died this past December one;
> Two children and a wife rapt in the cold,
> Three broken stares frozen in the sun
> Once four, now three, with thoughts of growing old.
> Alone at 5 A.M. his wife recalls
> Warm feet and arms protecting until six
> Or seven when he'd shadow on the walls
> Awake for eight, to build, to love, to fix.
> His January daughter Kim turns nine
> At ten she knows her dad is now retired.

Son Victor with eleven years behind
Turns twelve—the child is father of the sired.
Aorta rupture weakened brother's signs
A life cut off, reduced to fourteen lines.

Victor's funeral was held at St. Joseph's Church in Hammonton, New Jersey. One of his close friends came up to me at the funeral and said, "He thought a lot of you." I thought a lot of him, too, and remembered his telling me one day that his children were also mine. Maria and I have watched over his children, and their children, and the fourth generation of Walters. Victor and I were together during those early years when we slept together on the floor in a garage, when we roamed the streets and sand lots of Atlantic City, when I helped save his life after he jumped into the water so many years ago, and when Margie and I found him on the Nesco School playground and pleaded with Mother and Father Brown to have him come live with us so that we could all be together again. Comforting that there are deer etched into the granite on his tombstone. He loved them so. And we loved him.

Maria and I stayed in touch with Victor's wife Phyllis for many years until she passed away on January 31, 2012. Sometime after Victor's passing, she married Tony Azzara who also died before her. I spoke at her funeral.

Phyllis, a name from the Greek used by the poets meaning greenery. It suited her when you think about it. With her green thumb she was strongly influential in helping each of us grow as a family, from her own children to their children, helping to ease growing pains, nursing the sick, welcoming new additions to the family, standing as a matriarch always looking beyond herself and nurturing each of us fortunate enough to feel the impact of her greenery, her sunshine, her tears, her life-line as sister, mother, aunt, grandmother, and great-grandmother. How great she was but how modest. How lucky for us as we gathered together as family to break bread. How she loved Maria's mince pie, and how we loved her Johnny Cake and those unforgettable cookies and turkey with all the trimmings at Vic's and Donna's. And all that love, the hugs and kisses of all of us as we remember all her children and the good times, as we remember Vic and Tony. May she now rest in peace as we carry on in life remembering her smile, her humor, her kindness, and her courage in dealing with whatever hand she was dealt, using her unique green thumb to put things in place, to cultivate enduring values, and to instill a special joy and respect for life. How green is our valley because of her; it was the sweet things and memorable moments of our lives that Phyllis helped create. We will always miss her and love her.

Going back to the year 1973, Grandmother Louisa Craig, Mother Brown's and Aunt Hazel's mother, also passed away. My memories of her and Grandpa Tucker are special. They raised raspberries, and on one very hot July day I picked one hundred and six pints. In winter, Grandpa Tucker was bound to relive the impact of the great blizzard of 1888 when he was just a boy. Somehow I think he was always hoping for a good snowstorm. On an unusually warm winter's day, he would call the day a "weather breeder," anticipating a change in the forecast. I still use that term today. Grandmother Craig was an ardent reader, and Aunt Hazel and I would often sign out books from the library for her. Winter evenings were often spent playing dominoes in the kitchen, warmed by a pot-belly stove. Grandpa Tucker died chopping wood the same year Maria and I were married. Before Grandmother died, she gave me a small box of newspaper clippings about my accomplishments that she had collected over the years. At Christmas, I always create a special arrangement and place it on her gravesite. By the way, Grandmother Craig had the last word in her marriage. Grandpa Tucker's first wife was named Cora; Grandmother Craig made sure that she would be buried between Grandpa and his first wife!

Another extraordinary encounter heightened my senses as a prelude to what became my "end of summer" in 1974.

SUMMER'S OVER

An unexpected occurrence on the Atlantic City Expressway drove my summer away this year. It was touched off by a concentration of swallows, seemingly out of control, diving madly through the air at wide-eyed me behind a windshield. The swarm moved with dare-devil precision as a fleet of bombers whose design they had inspired. In flight, my mind flashed Hitchcock's bird screams. Gone. Then suddenly through a combination of life forces came the climax. There on the highway, in a small stretch of roadway, several hundred feet beyond the erratic air-borne swallows, lay hundreds of birds downed by some unexplained life force. To think that I had passed through that barrage of live birds, and neither auto nor bird collided. Perhaps they were preparing me for the funeral that lay ahead marking summer's end. Yet, I saw no undertakers nor flowers; I saw no police escort leading mourners to the cemetery. I saw only dead birds on cold concrete. I pained at the thought of spinning wheels crush-ing delicate, feathered bodies, stripping life of all its bloom. I hurt inside at the thought of a widespread killing frost that stills so completely. I reached for the poetry of wind currents that offer flight to beautiful autumn leaves, dead swallows reincarnated. Yesterday there were birds and summer. Today they are gone. At a loss, I reach for words and life forces to shape that which has taken flight.

Sadly, that "end of summer" occurrence was a prelude to other pain-ful moments for several of my Absegami students. One of my primary aims as a writing teacher was to encourage students to find their personal "voice" as writers.

A tragic car accident in the fall of 1975 prompted Frank Wesighan to write a deeply moving essay. I had kept his essay with a collection of student writing. Before including it in this memoir, I felt obliged to contact him for permission. Having heard that he was living in Florida, I used the internet to track him down. Finding a potential contact address, I sent the following e-mail on November 9, 2018:

> Frank,
>
> I am hoping you are the Frank Wesighan that I taught at Absegami High School in the early 1970's. My interest is that I am writing a memoir and planning to use the essay that Frank Wesighan wrote following that tragic accident wherein four Absegami football players lost their lives. The essay is entitled "Reflections from the Family," and I have kept it over the years because of its impact as a piece of writing. I remember you well as a student, and if you are the Frank Wesighan from Absegami, I would like your permission to use the essay in my memoir. Whoever you are, I hope you are well. I am now retired from Absegami. Please let me know the exact year of that dreadful accident that took the lives of Jimmy, Ronny, Mikey and Kenny.
>
> God bless.
> Sincerely,
> Dr. Daniel Walters

Within twenty-four hours, I had an e-mail from Frank:

> Dr. Walters: Great to hear from you! You were one of my favorite teachers of all time! Hope you are doing well. You had an impact on my life-you taught me to write with feeling and to look for the important things in life-family, friends, faith, etc. I am still in touch w several Absegami classmates and we talk about you when we get together- Craig Collins, Mike Wilkes, Cathy Keyes, Rick Krack. Yes, you can absolutely use that essay. I remember it was in the AC Press shortly after the accident. The accident was the fall of 1975

and we graduated in Spring 1976. It was one of the biggest tragedies of my life and I remember it whenever I see or hear of young people losing their lives in tragedy. We served as pall bearers for our friends and stayed in touch with their parents for several years. We still talk about our friends when we get together. Hope you and family are well. I married a teacher and one of my 3 daughters is a HS teacher. We have great respect for teachers-extremely hard workers and under-appreciated. If you would, please c-mail a copy of the article. Please also let me know when your book is published and how I can buy a copy. Great hearing from you. Please stay in touch! Thanks, Frank

REFLECTIONS FROM THE FAMILY

On Monday, September 29, four of my best friends in the whole world were taken away from me. All that I have left are many beautiful memories of the crazy things that Ronny, "Whale" (Jimmy), "Wolfgang" (Mike), and little Kenny used to do. Each one was an All-American boy in every sense of the word. And talk about smiles! In the four years that I have known them, I have yet to see them without the glowing faces that picked me up each and every day.

They were family to me. Our entire football team is one big family—happy at times, yes. But even more than that, we love each other—and are not the least bit afraid to express that love. There are very few people who can honestly appreciate what it means to hold hands in the huddle, or touch a team-mate's shoulder. They just don't understand. Well, we have been through many hard times and have come out as <u>ONE</u>. We have been tested and have come out <u>TOGETHER</u>.

This time will be no different. We will come through with our four friends right beside us. In the minds and hearts of our family, our brothers are still around and will always be with us. We must love each other and stick together even more than before…

As I see it, we should be mourning for ourselves, our family, and for those people who did not have the privilege of meeting my four friends. I know that God is taking care of them. They've got it made and are really better off than we are right now. We should cry only for those who remain.

In these times, God has exposed His might and is trying to sink a message into each of our hearts. My four friends have been a large price to pay merely to teach us something, but everything happens for a reason. You have got to believe that to make it through this life.

It is up to each individual to examine himself and realize what God is trying to tell him. Personally, all I keep thinking and hearing about is, "Man, I wish I had loved them more while they were here."

When I think of all the things we have been through, I realize that I have been taking my friends for granted all this time. I expected them to be around forever. Never in a million years could I have imagined that it was not to be. I just really didn't realize how lucky and privileged I was to know them until they were gone. For anyone listening, please don't fall into that trap: Love your friends to the fullest NOW!

I learned the most important lesson in life this week—something that school could not teach me: On that Monday I grew up and touched the real world for the first time. I realized that I cannot put off loving everyone around me for one minute longer. There can be no more waiting. I refuse to let myself say, "I should have…" or, "It could have been…" I must love all people <u>now</u> the way I should have loved my four friends <u>then</u>.

As my coach puts it, "There's only forty-eight minutes of football. No saving anything. You must go all out all the time, with every ounce of strength that you have."

Well, for me and for many members of our family, that says it all. Up until now, I have been guilty of saving something. I think we all have. I promise that I will never again make that mistake.

Thank you, Jimmy...and Ronny...and Mikey...and Kenny--- for everything.

Fellow teammate, friend and member of the Absegami Football Family-

Frank Wesighan #89

What a moving response and turning point in that young man's tribute to the loss of his four friends. Through honesty he captured the sentiments that many were feeling. It took exceptional courage to express the love he felt for his team and teammates. From his reflections emerge lessons for life, and for him the most important lesson: "On that Monday I grew up and touched the real world for the first time." What a powerful realization!

Another Absegami student's loss also expresses a powerful realization. She entitled her piece:

Thoughts On A Rainy Day

I've learned a lot in the past few days. I've learned that there comes a time when the whole world is a garish carnival mocking each tear as it trickles down my face. I've seen the birds turn traitor and the sun and moon become insensitive stoics who continue their thoughtless cycles when there is no longer any joy in them. I've felt the slow bitter death of happiness and hope that eats away the inner body, leaving only the dry husk to rustle in the wind. Macbeth hailed sleep as the balm of hurt souls, but sleep haunted by ragged visions is salt on an open wound. The acute loneliness of the week becomes unbearable when I know there is no weekend ahead when he will break the gloom with a kiss. But by far the worst are the memories. His knock on the door, the soft euphony of his voice, his shadow in all the places we frequented are all too vivid in my mind. Yes, I've learned a lot lately, and the one thing I've learned best is DEATH IS HELL—FOR THOSE WHO DON"T DIE.

Carefully chosen words, concrete images, and the literary allusion to Macbeth all contribute to this deeply felt loss of a loved one by a high school senior whose painful realization invites our empathy.

The final student selection for this chapter about coping with loss is a remarkable piece of writing, quite different from the previous two. The student's original version showed great promise, and my comments urging him to revise it resulted in what you see here.

OUR WOODS

Coming home from school on the bus, we passed the familiar stretch of woods I've known since I was six or seven years old. But there was something different about it. A large section was barren of trees, and where the trees once stood, now stood the yellow bulk of a bulldozer. To most of the kids on the bus, the sight had no real significance, but it brought about a panicky exchange of glances from several of my friends and me; for this was <u>our</u> woods.

We didn't legally own it, but, nevertheless, in our minds they were OUR woods and ours alone. Hidden among those trees were memories of hide-and-go-seek, and hikes and playing army and, above all, there was our clubhouse. It was a masterpiece of architecture for ten year olds, hidden high in a pine tree with invisibly skinny nails as rungs, so only the closest of inspections would discover our hideout.

All you needed was a peanut butter and jelly sandwich, a bottle of soda and a good friend, and you could spend the whole day up in the clubby talking about what happened in school that day or arguing about which of your favorite basketball teams was the best. But sometimes you just wanted to be alone. Maybe you had a fight with a friend or just felt really down; it didn't matter what; eventually you would end up at the clubby. Sometimes you'd meet somebody else there for the same reason as you; they had a problem. Talking to them magically made you feel a little bit better.

I haven't been to the clubhouse for a long time, but it would've been nice to try to recapture the good times that were patiently waiting for my return. It exists now only in the minds of us who once called it ours. And it will exist there only until some portion of our brains decides the space it occupies could be better used for something else. Then it will be torn down there too.

Those woods were a world for us. They would hide our actions from the outside world of ever-watching eyes and would not laugh when we confided in it our secret dreams: a new world, or soldiers stalking the enemy disguised as rabbits and birds, or anything else the mind could imagine. The woods were a friend, but the friendship has been broken by death. Maybe we should go to the now naked spot and say a prayer for our departed friend. But how do you bury an entire section of trees?

I'd like to write a real wow-o of an ending to make you feel really sad and break down and cry, but I doubt that anyone else but we who knew our woods so personally could feel the dying inside that we shared with the cracking and splintering of the trees that we knew so well.

David Warker

What a remarkable slice of life captured by a young man whose loss is as painful as that of a loved one. The concluding paragraph is powerful, perfectly echoing the personal loss of the young writer as the reader hears "the cracking and splintering of the trees."

I had also contacted David Warker on November 13, 2018, to request permission to use his essay. My e-mail to him read:

Dave,

I was able to track you down through Doug Collins. I am writing a memoir and would like to include a piece that you wrote in my Expository Writing class. The piece is entitled "Our Woods", and I have kept it all these years. It was a fine piece of writing back then and still is. If you are willing to have me use it in my memoir, please let me know.

Two days later I received the following e-mail from Dave:

Hello Dr. Walters. You are more than welcome to use anything I wrote in your class and I'm flattered you are even considering it. Your class was a favorite from high school, and I'm still a better writer because of it. And I thank you for that. I graduated in '78.

A fitting closing for this chapter takes me back to 1974 and a junior class that I was teaching Thornton Wilder's play, *Our Town*. That famous drama is divided into three sections: Act 1, The Daily Life; Act 2, Love and Marriage; and, Act 3, Death and Eternity. In keeping with the theme of this chapter, as my class and I moved toward the final act of the play, I asked them to bring in umbrellas for the cemetery scene. On a cold, damp November day, class members arrived with their umbrellas. Shortly after

I took roll, one of the students asked if I would go outdoors with them; they had something to show me. I accepted the request—a teacher must take chances, on occasion—and to my surprise, I was led down a pathway to a wooded area behind the school where the students had constructed the Grover's Corners Cemetery with headstones, dates, and inscriptions on tombstones for characters in the play. They had actually created the setting for the final act of the play, and they had done it on their own free time, on their days off from school. I was transfixed by the moment as we proceeded to act out the final scene of the play with umbrellas over our heads. Thinking back to what occurred, I am reminded again of those first graders in Massachusetts and The Day We Made the Sun. On this day, a group of high school juniors made their own "sun," uplifting the human spirit and echoing the Stage Manager's observation:

"There's something way down deep that's eternal about every human being."

Thornton Wilder (Act 3, **Our Town**)

17

ON TYPEWRITERS AND DISSERTATIONS

Typewriters have played a major role throughout the course of my life. As a writer, it makes sense that a mechanical machine, such as a type-writer, would be invaluable. In truth, I have done an enormous amount of long-hand writing with pens and pencils. Two special friends have given me beautiful writing instruments over the years: an Esterbrook pen from Franny Bell when I graduated from Glassboro State College, and a Pierre Cardin pen and pencil set from a personal friend, Joe Tozzi, sometime in the course of our thirty year relationship.

I have to say that using a pen or pencil gives me great pleasure and has been my preferred tool as an instrument for scribbling, creating, edit-ing, and refining thoughts, sermons, poems, essays, and note cards for research and, ultimately, for composing a lengthy dissertation.

Before I get to that dissertation and its remarkable evolution, let me chronicle a bit more about typewriters I have known. My earliest encoun-ter was the old Remington in the storeroom of the Old Union Hotel where, you will remember, I grew up with foster parents Dorothy and Bill Brown. As kids we often rummaged in that old storeroom which sat below the dance floor, you remember, where Joe Mulliner, that Tory refugee outlaw, was captured back in the 1770's. Anyway, finding that typewriter, which I am sure dates circa 1930, was a treasure to behold as we hauled it from the old storeroom to the round antique table in the dining room. I man-aged to revive the old gal and typed letters and papers on that archaic machine until it began to further decline, generally proving too old for the Twentieth Century.

Fortunately, my Aunt Hazel and Uncle Leo Landy purchased a Royal typewriter sometime in the mid 1950's. I was thrilled that they let me use it to type stories, essays, and my senior research paper on John Milton's **Paradise Lost**.

I was basically a hunt and peck typist since I did not take a formal typing class in high school. However, I think my piano and spelling skills helped a bit with my dexterity.

Over the years, I encountered the need for typewriters for college classes, lesson planning, and, of course, for my pre-doctoral dissertation work while at the university. That dissertation was the final hurdle for me to be awarded a doctoral degree in education. Luckily, I had a terrific contact at the university, Helene, a young woman who lived on Coca Cola and had hands of gold; she could type like nobody's business! She worked in the same office as Maria did at the School of Education at U/Mass. The only drawback was that once Maria and I moved back to New Jersey, Helene still resided in Amherst, Massachusetts. We had to work out a system for exchanging materials leading to the typing of a final copy. Before we could work out the system, I had a volume of writing to do which I had ignored, to some degree, because of my supervisory and teaching responsibilities at Absegami. Using a 1950's manual typewriter which Maria's family had purchased and she had used in high school and college, I had begun some work after we returned to New Jersey. Progress was slow, and I needed a push. That push came one day when Maria asked, "What do you need to finish your dissertation?" My response was immediate: "An electric type-writer." Eureka!

Within a few days Maria purchased a beautiful IBM Selectric typewriter, and I set myself to the task of completing the dissertation. I had already acquired approval for my topic and an outline of the overall structure and content of the chapters, along with hundreds of note cards taken during my research at the university and at other libraries, including the New York City Public Library. I also had accumulated a body of theoretical knowledge and practical experience through the Center for Aesthetic Education, course development and instruction, extensive reading, teaching experience, plus hard core data from my role as director of the Williamstown Integrated Arts Project. Synthesizing all of that was a major challenge which I managed to do, resulting in the completion of my dissertation. Periodic contacts with Helene involved reviewing and editing typed copy which she, in turn, typed in a polished, final form. Maria and I will never forget that final hour in August, 1974 when we transported copy for the dissertation to a printer in Northampton and then frantically drove back to Amherst while one of us inserted the pages in a black binder to meet a four o'clock deadline!

My dissertation committee included: Masha Rudman, Daniel C. Jordan, David Flight, David Day, and Dwight W. Allen, Dean, University of Massachusetts School of Education, all of whom approved the dissertation as to style and content in August, 1974. The title of my dissertation: Aesthetic Education: Its Aim Within The Context of An Integrated Arts Curriculum.

Who would have ever thought that a young boy making his way through the New Jersey State Child Welfare System would become a Doctor of Education? While pursuing that degree, I met and worked with some extremely gifted individuals, including one of my committee members, Dr. Daniel Jordan, whose life ended tragically. His influence, like that of many of the university staff and colleagues with whom I worked, continues to be felt. I also need to stress that I did not initially realize the significant impact that the Williamstown Integrated Arts Project would have on the development of my dissertation. My search for the primary aim of aesthetic education was realized, in large part, through practical applications in the project schools. I am deeply indebted to the project staff and the teachers and children of the project schools in the Berkshire communities for their contributions to my journey.

18

TEACHER OF THE YEAR NOMINATION AND OTHER ACHIEVEMENTS

The 1970's were coming to a close, and looking back I was amazed at what I had accomplished during the decade. With my graduate studies and dissertation complete, and my doctoral degree awarded, I actively pursued professional activities at both the local and state levels. Nominated to the Executive Board for the New Jersey Council Teachers of English, I traveled throughout the state participating in and conducting workshops. I also functioned as a liaison to the New Jersey Education Association's Affiliated Groups. My state affiliation connection helped me in planning and coordinating language arts workshops and conferences at both Stockton State College (now Stockton University) and Atlantic Community College (now Atlantic Cape Community College).

In 1974, I was invited to be an executive board member for the newly created New Jersey Alliance for the Arts. In that position, I was given a chance to assist in generating goals and planning regional and state conferences aimed toward formulating a comprehensive arts plan for the state of New Jersey. In 1977, I co-chaired a major arts conference at Middlesex County College. Overall, the alliance proved to be a viable extension of my work in aesthetics and the arts during my graduate studies at U/Mass and as the project coordinator for the Williamstown Integrated Arts Project.

In 1973-74, I had the distinct honor of being selected as an educator from the Northeast to be on the Task Force of the Southern Regional Educational Board in Atlanta, Georgia for which I presented a major position paper and collaborated with a myriad of educators exploring issues basic to teacher education in both pre-service and in-service settings. While in Atlanta, we had a snowstorm, and I had flown from Atlantic City to Atlanta. On the return trip from Atlanta to Atlantic City, I composed the following poem entirely while in flight:

LOOKING AT THE WORLD UPSIDE DOWN

Looking at the world upside down
Sun on the ground
Shadow 707 flying up aground;
Shapes I've never seen before
Whole rivers in a single sweep
Of the neck or an airline glance
Raising spirits turning around
In an upside-world-down dance.
Look at that river snaking its way
A winding eel tinseled by the sun
On the run looking at the world upside down.
Colors abound when you're upside down,
Spectruming from browns dissolving into
Grays spreading a flash of silver and golden haze.
There's an abstract painting of sublime design
Triangled shapes and drifting lines assuming
Unimaginable patterns of a mind upside-down
Drifting to the frozen north where flakes

Fell while I flew south.
A bird in flight
Snow makes me sing
I'm the sunlight in the sun
On that frozen lake below
A reflection of the daylight
On the deepening snow
About to descend while I'm still up!

Gotta hold on
Musn't cry
Reaching for a memory
In the shadow of my sky
Looking at the world upside down.
I'm down-
Snow deepens
Air thickens
Life quickens-
POSITION: UPRIGHT!

In 1975-76, I coordinated an in-service workshop on Censorship in Schools for the entire Oakcrest/Absegami faculty, with a particular emphasis on the implications of censorship for the English teacher. For that workshop, I was a facilitator, along with Dr. Ronald Ianonne and Dr. Robert Walker from West Virginia University in Morgantown.

In 1977, I was nominated as a candidate for the New Jersey Teacher of the Year Award which required a folio of materials, including a biography, philosophy of teaching, professional development activities, and educational/civic services. Although I was not the finalist in that competition, I was deeply moved by two letters of recommendation submitted to the committee by Absegami's Principal, Anthony Panarelle, and an Absegami colleague, George Johnston.

DANIEL N. WALTERS

Greater Egg Harbor Regional High School District

Mays Landing, New Jersey 08330

October 20, 1977

Re: Dr. Daniel Walters

To Whom It May Concern:

It is with a great deal of pride I recommend Dr. Daniel Walters as one of the best educators I have ever known. He is a person of exceptional integrity, creativeness and empathy which have made him a most successful teacher and supervisor in our system. He has accomplished so much that it would require pages of credits which I am certain you will see through information he will send you. However, I do want to emphasize a few accomplishments which have contributed immensely to our rather large English Department and to the entire District.

Dr. Walters was instrumental in creating and establishing a completely new English Department in a new school with its, our staff. He was instrumental in developing a quarter course program which has created and stimulated opportunities and interests for many youngsters. Dr. Walters, as a classroom teacher, is the perfect example of absolute dedication and delight. He has been able to extricate from any kind of student the ability and desire to want to read, write and speak with perfection and pride. It has been inspiring to me to observe the very positive attitude and love for learning this man has instilled in these youngsters.

Dr. Walters is strongly affiliated with local and state organizations in his quest to improve and make better the enitre area of language arts. He is always extremely active and provides all committees with much stimulation for improvement and change.

It is with pride I point out that Dr. Walters has received the rating of Outstanding Supervisor, a rating which is by no means liberally administered in this system.

If I were to elaborate further on the caliber of this candidate, it would never measure up or fully explain the magnitude of this super person and educator.

It is with a great deal of pleasure that I recommend Dr. Daniel Walters to you as one of the most outstanding educators in our school system. If I could be of any further assistance to you, please feel free to contact me at your convenience.

Very truly yours,

Anthony J. Panarelle
Principal

October 17, 1977

TO WHOM IT MAY CONCERN:

I have been advised that Dr. Daniel Walters has been nominated as a candidate for the Outstanding Teacher in the State of New Jersey. There is absolutely no doubt in my mind that Dr. Walters is deserving of this nomination. Why? Let me cite a few reasons:

About 14 years ago, as a student teacher, I had the privilege of observing Dan Walters at work in the classroom. I saw a young, curly-haired dynamo of energy motivating students in a manner almost impossible to describe. He was everywhere at once—up this aisle, down another—and the youngsters in that room could not help but get caught up in his dynamism. The subject of that lesson was Shakespeare, but I doubt that even John Geilgud could have matched Dan's enthusiasm, vitality, and knowledge.

As a student teacher, I left that classroom with but one thought in mind: I was going to be a teacher like Mr. Walters. I'm still trying.

A few years after that initial meeting, I was fortunate enough to obtain a teaching position in Oakcrest High School. Dan Walters was now my colleague! During those somewhat hectic and precarious early years, Dan came to my aide almost daily. When I needed help with a lesson, he was there to give advice and encouragement, and when I really got stuck, he would take time out to come into my classroom and "team teach." I guess you might say he was my idol.

During the past five years, Dan has been my department chairman. Working with him is both a joy and a constant challenge. The joy comes from his sparkling, mischievous personality. His wit and humor are equal to his intellectual capacity. He has an unabashed love for humanity, which includes those of us in the English department. What other educational leader would pick a bouquet of wild-flowers and personally give one to each member of his staff as a reminder that "Spring is Here!"

His love for people, however, is more evident in the classroom than anywhere else. He loves his kids, and I have witnessed ample evidence that his students return that love. His humane sensitivity and understanding have, on many occasions, inspired an otherwise distraught and depressed youngster to keep trying. As one young man said to me just a few weeks ago, "If it weren't for Dr. Walters, I would've quit this place long ago."

Does Dan Walters get my vote? If it were possible, I'd stuff the ballot box!

Respectfully,

George M. Johnston
English Teacher
Absegami High School

I was both flattered and humbled by the letters of recommendation from Anthony Panarelle, Principal, and George Johnston, English teacher colleague. To this day I hold both of them in high esteem for their support and professionalism.

Throughout the overall decade, I was further honored by a number of national organizations:

Outstanding Secondary Educator (1974)

Outstanding Leader in Elementary & Secondary Education (1976)

Outstanding Young Man of America (1977)

I would be remiss in not mentioning the national recognition that came to two Absegami students through the 1977 Scholastic Writing Awards Competition. Competing in a field of over 25,000 students, Barbara Szlanic, a freshman, placed second as a national winner for her essay, ***So You Want To Be A Hockey Player***. Also, Tracy Miller, a senior, was awarded an honorable mention for her essay, ***Reading Avenue Fantasy***.

Of the numerous honors I received, the one that pleased me most came in October, 1979, when the National Council Teachers of English commended the Absegami English Department for excellence in its instructional program by its evident contribution to the high quality of writing of its one or more students honored with the National Council Teachers of English Achievement Awards in Writing.

1979 was a pivotal year for Absegami as voters went to the polls and approved a referendum to build Absegami High School in Galloway Township. The referendum passed by one vote, as mentioned in Chapter 15. Although we supervisors had submitted preliminary plans for departmental and building specifications in the construction of the new school, there was major work to be done, and September, 1982, was not too far away; that was the date for the long-awaited opening of an independent Absegami High School. As Absegami Braves, we were ready to don our feathered headdresses and board our canoes after what had been a lengthy ten-year attachment!

19

MIDDLE STATES REVIEW, RONALD GRUNSTRA, SUMMER SLIPS AWAY, AND A SOVEREIGN CRICKET

Over the next three decades, the nature of my supervisory role expanded. Initially, I was hired as an English teacher and department chairman overseeing English and Reading staff members. As time passed, my responsibility grew; I became the supervisor of the Foreign Language Department, along with the two departments I was already handling. The Foreign Language Department was a joy to supervise. Donna Anderson, a French teacher, was Absegami's first teacher of the year, and Irene Fineberg, a gifted German teacher, was recognized by Princeton University for Excellence in Teaching. Not knowing how far the administration would stretch me, I found myself in charge of five departments when I retired in 2005: English, Reading, Media, Drama and Dance.

Besides Anthony Panarelle, I worked under five different principals during my tenure at Absegami: Ronald Grunstra, Lynne Basner Gale, Dan Mackie, Michael Carr, and Raymond Dolton. Each played a unique role in the evolution and expansion of Absegami High School. Ron Grunstra, whom I called Mr. G, led the transition to the new Absegami in Galloway Township. You may remember in Chapter 15 of this memoir that he was one of the chiefs who helped break ground for the school. It wasn't long after we had staked our claim that the school was scheduled for a Middle States Review. It was Mr. Grunstra who asked me to serve as master of ceremonies for that Middle States Review dinner where I assumed the role of the Stage Manager from the play *Our Town* and talked about our history, equating our beginnings with Noah's Ark as we found ourselves docked together with Oakcrest High School for what turned out to be a ten year coupling.

Allow me to take you back to that Middle States Review dinner in 1985 and share some additional excerpts from the presentation I gave:

> Good evening. It is my pleasure to welcome all of you to our town. Post Office: Absecon (long "e" and an accent on the second syllable) for those who know how to say it, or Absecon (short "e" with an accent on third syllable) for those who don't! We're located in Galloway Township, Atlantic County, State of New Jersey, the United States of America, Continent of North America. Longitude: 39.4 Degrees North…Latitude: 74 Degrees West. They are our vital statistics except for one more, in particular, that sums up who we are and where we are in that broad expanse of time and space: Absegami High School, Cornerstone, 1982. Dreams are the stuff that life is made of, and after a rash of fitful activity, Absegami High School became a reality. The building was dedicated with all the hoopla that goes with ceremonies like that. Mighty proud we are of this institution, its Board of Education, administration, dedicated teaching staff, parents of our students and the students themselves who travel here by bus from Egg Harbor City, Washington Township, Port Republic, and Galloway Township schools, particularly Arthur Rann School just down the road apiece—make a right on Eighth Avenue. Right nice bunch of students here—well-behaved for the most part; Mr. David Dunlevy, our Vice-Principal sees to that. Bright enough for all normal purposes, our students particularly enjoy lunch and physical education while struggling with their academics and participating in a variety of extra-curricular activities. Quite a few of our students manage to distinguish themselves in one way

or another. A young orator, Gary Melton, was a state finalist in the American Legion Oratorical Contest this past year; and, Alythea McKinney, a senior, is being honored this year through the National Council Teachers of English as an outstanding writer, one of 800 from across the country—quite a distinction! I taught both Gary and Alythea. Naturally, we place a high value on academic achievement for which individual students are awarded the Principal's Medallion for excellence at the awards assembly in June for outstanding performance in English, Industrial Arts, Physical Education, Business Education, Foreign Language, Music, Special Education, Media, Drama and Art. A lot of time and effort go into earning that medallion, into realizing and developing human potential. Perhaps that's the eternal part of us that Mr. Grunstra and the others were trying to dig up back on the day of Absegami's groundbreaking and dedication. Our aspirations as teachers were high, then, and continue to be as we go about our business preparing lesson plans and activities to shape the minds, bodies, spirits and human potential of those delightful youngsters who made us laugh, and think, and dream, and hope—and, on occasion, cry. A lot of laughter, thinking and dreaming have brought us to this moment in time in our town and its school. In closing, I hope that those of you who have come to take a snoop, snoop well; for there's a lot to see in what Absegami is and is becoming. With that in mind, it is my pleasure to introduce our illustrious principal, Chief Silver Fox himself, Mr. Ronald Grunstra.

Mr. Grunstra would remain Absegami's principal for seven years after I made that presentation on the evening of the Middle States Review Dinner. He had sent me a complimentary note about that evening. In turn, I made a copy of my original presentation, along with the following afterward which I gave him when he was about to retire:

In a few hours the sun will go down on our town for today, February 28, 1992. There are a few harbingers of spring in the air: my crocuses are up, and some jonquils in a warmly protected area of the yard are in bud. Several years have passed since that Middle States presentation recounted above occurred; a number of classes have graduated; many awards have been granted; Absegami has been transformed through building additions and extensions. A good bushelful of all the good things we've reaped over the years can be credited to the leadership and humanity of Mr. Grunstra, our principal who is about to retire. Absegami just won't be the same without him. They do say that the morning star gets wonderful bright just before sun-up. I would predict that it might be just a little less bright until we make the adjustment here at Absegami. It takes time to readjust when a teacher, principal and friend like Mr. G (that's how I sometimes address him) takes his leave. But then, who could ever forget the brightness that he brought to that morning star—I'd call it first magnitude!

Another first magnitude star in Maria's and my life was her mother Jennie DiGiovanni who passed away in December, 1985. Maria and I had been married twenty-one years when her mother passed; it was a difficult Christmas. Coping with her passing was painful, and although I did not give a eulogy at her funeral, I composed a summer's ending piece dedicated to her memory in September, 1986.

AS SUMMER SLIPS AWAY

Maria asked the other day, "Aren't you going to write about your end of summer this year?" I told her, "I've been thinking about it." And one night, not long after her question, upon teaching an SAT class at Absegami, the pieces for my "end of summer" came together. It climaxed tonight just as I was leaving school at 9:10 P.M., September twenty-third, after my first SAT session. SAT— Scholastic Aptitude Test. SAT—Summer's All Through. SAT— Summer's Autumn Thunder.

Yes, summer's autumn thundered as I opened the door to a late summer, early autumnal storm arrival: a woman seeking her child. As she entered the school building, she exclaimed, "Oh, a frog!" And, there on the terrazzo floor was a leaping frog whose peculiar presence in an institution of higher learning forced me into a frog-like position as I sought to capture the end-of-summer critter as one season hopped away and another leaped in. Down in a haunch I grabbed for the toad, managing a catch after three laughable leap frogs. The lady walked on down the hallway as I deposited Froggie outside and hopped through puddles and rain-drops to my car. Consciously, I smelled my hand, searching for that remembered scent when boyhood days had prompted treks into swamps in search of tadpoles and plump bog frogs with bulging eyes, blowing bubbles and wetting hands, causing warts and that remembered scent that wasn't there tonight when I sniffed to find it.

Gone. Now that summer's over, my memory searched for that scent and the reality of things passing from my life at this summer's end. They were clarified by the tropical-like rain that drenched car and roadway as I drove home to A.C., alone. Arriving home, I found Maria's note: "Gone to a movie for a change." No one home.

A year ago Maria's mother would probably have been asleep in her favorite chair as the television transmitted images lost in space.

She died last December rendering a change of season in our lives, one that blurred the passage of winter, spring and summer.

A person's passing, I've come to find, may render one mute to the subtle changes of a passing season. Such was the effect of Jennie's demise. Bigger than life, more lovely than a summer's day, more vibrant than the most regal flower of my summer garden, or a leaf ablaze with autumn's color pressed between the covers of an ancient book—Jennie. So pressed, that leaf will retain a certain slant of sunlight prompting, perhaps, a montage of images capturing summer's end, autumn's beginning, Jennie's living and dying—a collection of cyclical events ranging from birth to death as Maria and I gasped at the reality and pain of Nature's twists in our dying and crying.

SAT—sad at times, but after great pain, dulled senses awaken to find vestiges of hope and meaning and a will to go on. The feelings, I suppose, never fully go away. Rainy days of summer and autumn's pageantry deepen the colors of life and death, giving a clarified meaning to mankind's comings and goings. "The Celebrated Jumping Frog of Calaveras County"—thank you, Mr. Twain. The Celebrated Life of Jennie DiGiovanni, Madame Butterfly. Little lady with a suitcase longing for a summer season to sell her linens by the seashore.

The tide has gone out. My frog has leaped away. Jennie sleeps; Maria weeps. That feeling will subside—just a little—as summer slips away.

That line from the above tribute, "...a leaping frog whose peculiar presence in an institution of higher learning forced me into a frog-like position," transported my mind back to another end of summer recollection written shortly after an evening walk down Sovereign Avenue in Atlantic City. I shared it with Irene Fineberg, the German teacher mentioned earlier, as we drove to school together the morning after I had composed the piece. Mrs Fineberg actually lives on Sovereign Avenue. And so, another "end of summer" reflection:

A SOVEREIGN CRICKET

A Sovereign Avenue gutter cricket chirped the ending to a song for me tonight. It's amazing how much I have come to depend on lowly creatures for significant messages like that. It makes crickets and related creatures somewhat higher than lower, I suppose. Now, I don't mean to imply that I read CRICKET, or that I know the Cricket Alphabet, or that that sovereign cricket cricked a song. But, the chirp coming tonight communicated. It was as if the insect had been cued to sound the final note rounding out a summer symphony. Other sounds of that symphony, harsher ones, are memories now: the cacophony of screaming kids on their way to Sovereign Avenue beach, or quarrelsome sidewalk parents—imports from bigger cities and towns—resorting to parental tactics: yelling to hear themselves yell—more like crows than crickets! Or, the unforgettable pitches of ice cream beach vendors, a block and a half away, who outdid parents, kids and crickets with their "Getch your fudgie-wudgies right here!" Add to that clamor the roaring gossip whispered under fading umbrellas and shaded faces, along with kids-in-tantrum under the sun who either didn't get fudgie, or did, and dropped him in the sand—poor little sand-dears whose castles melted away, transforming them into beach monsters who compete with high-pitched glares and aging stuffed baked potatoes for fathers who steam in the sun reminding mother, "He's your son!" What a symphony! Somewhere there must be a resolution. There is. It began when beaches and streets, like Sovereign Avenue, were left to Geiger-counter operators who searched quietly for coins, jewels, and unexpected finds—non-verbal leftovers of beachcombers and sidewalk Annies far enough away now so that the symphony's resolution could be heard. It resolved itself tonight when Cricket chirped the closing. I heard it soft and clear. My senses, fully awake, interpreted its song: Frost forms. Skies crystal. Leaves color. Birds migrate.

Cricket chirps the end of summer!

PEOPLE IN HIGH PLACES

That Sovereign Cricket clicked in my mind a series of memorable events and links to people in high places. I can still see and hear President Ronald Regan pleading with the Russian premier, "Mr. Gorbachev, tear down that wall!" President Regan's successor, George H.W. Bush, lit up the country with his thousand points of light marking 1989, the year he assumed office, as the end of the Cold War. I included both Presidents Reagan and Bush in a poem I wrote on September 6, 1989. I wasn't angry with either President, but the poem conveys a harsh message echoing my personal struggle thinking back to the day our mother Madeline abandoned us, not because of cocaine but for reasons I'll never know.

ABANDONED BABIES OF COCAINE-
ADDICTED MOTHERS
I wonder where the President was
When my mother abandoned me?
Would have been nice to have had
The Presidential seal of approval
Or disapproval
As she deserted
The three of us
Back in the mid 1940's.
I wonder what she was hooked on
Unfree, strung out, habituated to

A life of unfulfilled dreams
Mired in a rut?
Where, then, were the police,
Politicians
Agencies of the free world,
Department of Human Welfare,
Executive Branch of the U.S. government
When she deserted us
Addicted
To a never-ending search for reasons?
That was then; this is now:
Roosevelt
    Truman
        Eisenhower
           Kennedy
              Johnson
           Nixon
        Ford
    Carter
Reagon

We may have gotten more than
Expected in this election:
Hold on tight to those abandoned babies
Of cocaine-addicted mothers, Mr. Bush!

President George H.W. Bush authorized military operations in Panama which the United States invaded in December 1989, three months after I had composed my poem. The invasion led to overthrowing Panama's corrupt dictator, Manuel Noriega who was threatening the security of Americans living there, and—here is the clincher—trafficking drugs to the United States. Thank you, Mr. Bush, for your actions may very well have helped curtail drug traffic to America and reduce the number of abandoned babies and cocaine-addicted mothers.

A month before President George H.W. Bush invaded Panama, I received a congratulatory letter from the State of New Jersey Office of the Governor on November 27, 1989. At the time, the governor was the Honorable Thomas H. Kean. Governor Kean's letter helped to validate my continued professional growth, commitment to the teaching profession, and contributions to the youth of our community.

STATE OF NEW JERSEY
OFFICE OF THE GOVERNOR
CN-001
TRENTON
08625

THOMAS H. KEAN
GOVERNOR

November 27, 1989

Dr. Daniel Walters
Absegami
201 South Wrangleboro
Absecon, New Jersey 08201

Dear Dr. Walters:

I was delighted to learn that one of your students won an Achievement Award in Writing from the National Council of Teachers of English. As a former teacher, I know how proud you are of Jason Merkoski.

While winning this special award is a great honor for Jason, it also reflects upon your skills as a teacher. I commend you for your dedication, and I join the Council in applauding your commitment to the education of our youth.

All the best.

Sincerely,

Tom Kean

Thomas H. Kean
Governor

Several years after the letter I received from Governor Kean, I received another letter of some distinction; it was a letter dated November 25, 2002 from The White House, from Desiree Thompson, Special Assistant to President George W. Bush, the son of former President George H.W. Bush. The White House correspondence grew out of a writing prompt and competition I helped initiate for high school seniors who had attended Margate City schools. That competition had its roots in the Margate Fall Funfest, a non-profit activity celebrating the city of Margate each September with food vendors, juried artisans, pumpkins, chrysanthemums, haystacks, cornstalks, and live music. The seed for the Funfest came from Joe Tozzi, a local business man and president of the Margate Business Association. Mr. Tozzi teamed up with my wife Maria, and after extensive planning and meetings with Margate's city fathers and with a former student of Maria's,

Larry Higbee, who created a skillfully drawn blueprint of the bay area site proposed for the festival, approval was granted and the Margate Fall Funfest debuted in September, 1998.

Since its inception, the Margate Fall Funfest has awarded over $100,000 in scholarships which takes us back to a letter from the White House thanking me for a letter I had sent to President George W. Bush. Along with my letter to the President was a copy of Karine Hyman's winning essay from the 2002 scholarship competition sponsored through the Margate Fall Funfest. That competition challenged students to write a letter to President George Bush in answer to his call for volunteerism.

THE WHITE HOUSE
WASHINGTON

November 25, 2002

Daniel N. Walters, Ed.D
Chair
Margate Fall Funfest
   2002 Scholarship Program
Margate City, New Jersey

Dear Dr. Walters:

Thank you for your letter to President Bush and for sharing Karine Hyman's essay.

The President believes that one of our most important responsibilities as citizens is to give something back to our communities and to make them better places for everyone to live. You have answered that call by inspiring our young people to volunteer and improve the lives of fellow citizens.

A letter from President Bush has been sent to Karine.

Laura joins me in sending our best wishes.

Sincerely,

Desiree Thompson
Special Assistant to the President
and Director of Presidential Correspondence

Maria and I spent over fifteen years in leadership and volunteer roles for the Margate Fall Funfest. In our final year, the organization named the scholarship program after us, the Margate Business Association's Daniel and Maria Walters Scholarship. We continue to develop an annual writing prompt for the essay portion of the scholarship program, along with all aspects of judging, leading to the awarding of scholarships to finalists living in Margate City or Longport, New Jersey.

My continuing search for people in high places takes me back to my boyhood days at the Hilda S. Frame School on June 2, 1953. That was the day of Queen Elizabeth II's coronation at Westminster Abbey in London, England. We watched the coronation on a black and white television set that our school had purchased by collecting boxtops from cereal boxes. The entire community kicked in to gather those boxtops. I was fascinated with the pomp and circumstance that accompanied the coronation. My interest in the Royal Family has never waned.

That brings me to August 31, 1997 when Diana Spenser, married to Queen Elizabeth's son Charles, died from wounds suffered in a car crash at the Pont de l'Alma Road Tunnel in Paris, France. In both life and death, Diana had touched the hearts of millions. Deeply moved by her untimely death, I composed the following tribute.

A SPENSERIAN STANZA

Writer's block has kept me from
Setting pen to paper until now.
So many words and tears shed
For the Princess of Wales
In the streets, the press, the media
In all of those Books of Condolences
The world wails for the Princess of Wales
Whose estrangement from the Royalists
Only endeared her more to the Loyalists.
An untimely death has united a nation;
Diana's beauty and life's story have been
Chronicled and photographed day by day
Capturing her shyness in love, marriage
To Charles, births of William and Harry,
Separation and divorce and tragic demise.
Oh, where, where is that kiss that could
Awaken a sleeping princess?
The House of Windsor is tumbling down,

Tumbling down, tumbling down
Wordsworth's London is about to drown
In all of those tears from all of those
Commoners whose words of condolence elevate

DIANA

On a not so merrie September sixth millions
Viewed the procession to Westminster Abbey
In a mourning tide of heavy hearts
As William and Harry struggled for the
Privacy their mother never had, not even now,
As her children struggled with adolescent and
Child-like grief, human pain without mother,
Longing to wake up to a happy ending.
The House of Windsor is tumbling down;
Wordsworth's London is about to drown
Longing for the Princess to wake up,
The Queen of the people's hearts
Whose presence, empathy and humanity
Sparked a ray of hope in a world of gloom,
A magical princess who used her title
To ease pain and hurt while walking with
Kings but never losing the common touch.
Sadly, in her final hour she emerged a
Human Sacrifice leaving the world a better
Place and the course of England's monarchy
 Forever altered.

The House of Windsor is tumbling down
The House of Windsor is tumbling down
The House of Spenser is gaining ground
And the rest is silence.

I end this chapter with one final recollection of a luminary who might be considered in a high place. Let me set the stage before revealing the identity of our 4 North Montpelier Avenue Atlantic City Christmas dinner house guest sometime in the mid 1970's. The guest, a close friend and collaborator with Maria's brother Paul, was a celebrated British writer who we learned had requested roast goose for Christmas dinner. The request led to a sort of tug-of-war on Christmas Day between the cook, my wife Maria, and our guest, a famous playwright. Tension arose between the two as Maria had stuffed the goose, set the timer and temperature, and placed the bird in the oven after which our dinner guest made frequent visits to the kitchen for the purpose of either raising or lowering the oven temperature of the roasting goose. At one point, when Maria's temperature had risen along with the internal temperature of the roasting goose, she turned to Peter Shaffer and firmly said, "Mr. Shaffer, I would not begin to tell you how to write a play, and I respectfully request that you leave the cooking of the goose to me!"

In the end, the goose was a triumph, and Mr. Shaffer proclaimed the stuffing of the bird a crowning glory! A memorable dinner, overall, it served as a thank you to a very gifted playwright whose major dramas included **Black Comedy**, **Equus** and **Amadeus**, all which Paul, Maria, Mother Jennie, and I saw on opening nights in New York City. How thrilling to have been in such company, and to have met several luminaries, including Anthony Hopkins, Geraldine Page, Lynn Redgrave, and Peter Firth.

Before his death at the age of ninety on June 6, 2016 (coincidentally, June 6 was the birthday of Hilda S. Frame), our dinner guest was knighted by Queen Elizabeth II in 2001, dubbing him Sir Peter Shaffer.

21

A MAN FOR ALL SEASONS

I can still hear Maria's brother Paul Giovanni singing the "Soliloquy" from Rodgers and Hammerstein's **Carousel**. How he loved musicals! I can also hear him singing at our wedding in 1964 as he serenaded us with the beautiful ballad, "Try to Remember," from **The Fantasticks**, the longest running play in New York in which he played the Boy in the original New York production. That play is particularly special to Maria and me as we first met at a production of **The Fantasticks**, directed by her brother in August, 1963, at the Gateway Playhouse in Somers Point, New Jersey.

Paul was an exceptionally gifted actor, musician, composer, playwright, and director. His collaboration with Peter Shaffer led to Paul's directing Shaffer's **Black Comedy** and **White Liars** as well as staging Britain's first national tour of **Amadeus**. I am sure that much was learned about the writing craft through the collaborative work of two highly creative talents. Peter was honored with both Tony and Academy Awards. In 1979, Paul also garnered a Tony nomination for directing **The Crucifer of Blood**, his original Broadway play which debuted on September 28, 1978, starring Paxton Whitehead and Glenn Close. The play, a Sherlock Holmes mystery, was nominated for four Tony Awards and won a Lighting Design Award for Roger Morgan; it also received the Los Angeles Drama Critics Circle Award for Special Visual and Sound Effects after premiering at the Ahmanson Theatre where Jeremy Brett played Dr. Watson. Paul also directed The **Crucifer of Blood** in London at the Theatre Royal Haymarkets in 1979 where it ran for 397 performances. Before the New York production,

Crucifer was presented at the Buffalo Studio Area Theatre where Paul purchased a fur coat because of the brutal cold. Naturally, Maria, Mother Jennie and I had special seating for the Broadway opening night at the Helen Hayes Theatre. Bravo!

In addition to his theatrical performances and productions, Paul was also an accomplished musician, creating music and lyrics for the haunting film, *The Wickerman*, for which he was credited with creating perfectly crafted music for what continues to be a highly regarded cult film. Besides that film credit, he composed original music for the 1971 production of Shakespeare's *Twelfth Night,* directed by Jeff Bleckner, at the Arena Stage in Washington, D.C.. He also recorded *Sideshow*, an album of ten original songs, seven of which he had a major hand in composing.

To me, Paul became the brother that I had lost in 1973. To Maria, he was both big brother and hero whom she adored. Sadly, he died on June 17, 1990 at the age of fifty-seven. I celebrated him in eulogy:

> In the play *Equus* which Peter Shaffer dedicated to Paul,
> a young boy is the focal subject of a haunting drama that
> punctuates the idea that materialism and convenience have
> destroyed man's capacity for worship and passion. A fitting
> tribute to Paul, to have had the play dedicated to him, and,
> later, to have directed it; for he himself—a living antithesis of
> that play's theme—was essentially a man with deep feelings,
> thoughts and emotions—a man of passion. His passion for
> the theatre and life was marked by an exceptional sensibility
> and artistic flair that enabled him to make us think, laugh
> and cry. The Giovanni signature as director and performer
> evolved through a sharp wit, penetrating intelligence, and
> good old-fashioned hard work. He seemed to have a passion
> for hard work. I'm sure that he believed you can't wait for
> inspiration; you have to go after it with a club. That's pas-
> sionate! His driving desire to clarify or distill the essence of a
> character, scene, or play enabled him to connect with audi-
> ences, to move beyond the humdrum, to elevate the human

spirit, to lift us up when we were feeling down, to communicate the language of Shakespeare or a Chekov, and somehow, magically, to change our lives, to stir our passions. Artists do things like that. Yes, Paul was an artist whose love for the theatre involved a process of singular magnitude and integrity as he struggled with words and images, sounds, settings and characters aiming to transform that elusive space, the stage, into a collection of memorable scenes, acts, costumes, drama, lighting and pageantry raised to a level of significant form that often left us, his audience, breathless. And, breathless he must have left his audience at the University of South Carolina in the final scene of Chekov's play, **The Three Sisters**. In that scene, Olga puts her arms around both her sisters and says:

> *Our faces and our voices will be forgotten and people won't even know that there were once three of us here. But our sufferings may mean happiness for the people who come after us. There will be a time when peace and happiness reign in the world and then we shall be remembered kindly and blessed. No, my dear sisters, life isn't finished for us yet. We're going to live. The band is playing so cheerfully and joyfully. Maybe if we wait a little longer we shall find out why we live, why we suffer. Oh, if we only knew, if only we knew.*

CHEKOV. Three Sisters (Act 4)

And breathless, too, he left us with that resounding thunder and lightning storm in his **Crucifer of Blood**. He told Maria and me that the inspiration for that thunder and lightning storm came from his memory of intense storms at the Jersey shore in Atlantic City when he was growing up.

Shakespeare might have been writing about Paul when Hamlet, in Act II, Scene 2, speaks:

What a piece of work is man/how noble in reason/
how infinite in faculties/in form and moving how
express and admirable/in action how like an angel/
in apprehension how like a god/the beauty of the world/
the paragon of animals.

The ghost of Hamlet's father passionately pleads to his son,

"Remember me."

Paul "El Guyo" Giovanni passionately sang to his audience, "Try to remember…"

How could we possibly forget this Man For All Seasons!

* *

Deep in December it's nice to remember
Without a hurt, the heart is hollow.
"Try to Remember" (from ***The Fantasticks***)

Maria's Brother Paul Giovanni

(22)

STORM CHASER

That staged thunder and lightning storm in Paul's play, ***The Crucifer of Blood***, stirred my long-time fascination with meteorology and storms. I wasn't aware of any evidence of the Great Atlantic Hurricane of 1944 when I arrived by train from Baltimore to Atlantic City sometime after that storm. It had caused extensive damage along the East Coast, ripping apart Atlantic City's famed Boardwalk, destroying Heinz Pier, and flooding Convention Hall, severely damaging the world's largest pipe organ. The aftermath of that hurricane played on my mind as a nine year old when my sister Margie and I moved to Nesco in 1949 to live with the Browns. You'll remember my interest in that huge plank propped up against the maple tree in the backyard. Winds from the 1944 hurricane, over a hundred miles east of the Browns' residence, had caused that tree to buckle. Seeing that plank up against the tree was like having the Great Atlantic Hurricane of 1944 in my own backyard.

I love wind and rain. What fun I had as an amateur meteorologist using a map of the Atlantic Basin to track tropical systems that traveled from the Cape Verde Islands through the Caribbean and into the Gulf of Mexico, or up the Eastern Seaboard. I didn't want anyone to get hurt or to die; I was simply intrigued with the structure, power and impact of storms.

They didn't begin naming hurricanes until 1953, and lo and behold they named one Hazel. Of course all of Nesco was astir since my Aunt Hazel Landy was affectionately referred to by her husband Leo as both a barracuda and a hellion! Uncle Leo declared that Hurricane Hazel would be one for the books. Well, the storm certainly made my Aunt Hazel a local celebrity, and although the storm did little damage to our town, Aunt Hazel reported that the storm had taken down a tree up at Essie Briegel's house. Elsewhere, Hazel proved to be the deadliest and costliest storm of the 1954 Hurricane Season; I guess Uncle Leo was right although I would say that both Hazels were ones for the books!

Another extremely dangerous hurricane named Donna was the strongest of the 1960 Atlantic Hurricane Season. I recall being in the kitchen with Mother Brown talking about the eye of the storm which was predicted to pass over the East Coast. My excitement about Donna led to a poetic creation:

DONNA

Her fury descended upon the Isles
In a capricious journey of uncertain miles
Destructive gales with driving rains
Causing hardship and widespread pains
For the destined who lay in her fickle path
Searching for places to strike her wrath.
Brutally, uncaringly, inciting fear
Creating havoc stressing her tear
Of power and strength and driving force—
People praying that she would change course.
And thus because of an unlady-like air
She continued erratically to plant despair
For those unfortunates lying ahead
Some of whom now lie dead.
Where will she go? I feel her hurry
Tropical Donna only willing to bury
The land with water and traces
Hopefully receding as she races
To a favored area, whatever it may be,
As the Isles and miles brace for Sister E.

Besides Hazel and Donna, I remember tracking Allen, Connie, Diane, Camille, Floyd, Gloria, Hugo, Irene, Isabel, Andrew and Katrina, among others. And, of course, there was Superstorm Sandy in October, 2012, which ravaged sections of New Jersey, forcing us to evacuate our home in Margate for three days. Overall, we were very lucky since we missed the brunt of the storm. However, numerous businesses and homes in Margate, Longport, Ventnor, and Atlantic City were seriously compromised. One house on our street had to be leveled because of water and infrastructural damage. In some areas of Central and North Jersey, damage was far more severe, surpassing that caused by a ferocious three day March Nor'easter that hit the Jersey shore in 1962.

I was a senior at Glassboro State College that year and recall friends of mine in the dorm talking about a storm raging at the Jersey shore. I had just gotten out of the infirmary following a bout with the flu. I remember rain changing to huge snowflakes in Glassboro. Maria and I had not yet met, but she later told me that she had over twenty inches of snow at Cabrini College in Radnor, Pennsylvania from the same storm. Her mother was living in Atlantic City where they had declared martial law because of the flooding and damage from the three-day nor'easter. Maria managed to get home with a friend who had driven her; she talked her way into being allowed into the city since they were not allowing anyone in or out.

Before the week was out, Tom Wriggins, a college friend of mine, asked if I wanted to take a drive to Ocean City where his parents lived. Storm-chaser that I was, I accepted the invitation immediately. What I saw when Tom and I arrived was unbelievable. Ocean City looked like a war zone with tons of sand piled ten or more feet high; overturned homes were off their foundations. There was debris everywhere. That 1962 extra-tropical March storm is said to have reconfigured the shape of the eastern coastline from Florida to Maine. What a storm! One for the books, as Uncle Leo would say.

I remember a day in late October, twenty-nine years after that 1962 storm. I had tried several ways to get home to Margate before I finally found an outlet via the Atlantic City Expressway. All of the routes I had tried were impassable because of rising water, the result of tidal flooding caused by what has come to be known as the 1991 Halloween No-Name Storm. That storm did finally acquire an identity through the skilful depiction of what Sebastian Junger called *The Perfect Storm*, a powerful non-fiction story of men against the sea, specifically the crew of the Andrea Gail who had sailed out of Gloucester Harbor, Massachusetts, ending up victims of a monster North Atlantic nor'easter. Junger's thrilling account of the storm and the crew of the Andrea Gail was not published until 1997.

The actual storm originated from a Category 2 Hurricane named Grace which dissipated somewhere in the South Atlantic, but its remnants regenerated resulting in the formation of what became the Perfect Storm which it is believed contained at its core a newly developed cyclone which blossomed into a catastrophic nor'easter without a name.

Looking back before Junger's 1997 publication of *The Perfect Storm*, I recall standing on a Margate beach in 1991 imagining the fifteen to thirty feet waves off the coast that I had been hearing about on numerous weather reports associated with the developing storm impacting the entire East Coast from Canada to Florida. The powerful storm created extremely high tides, winds and beach erosion, and interestingly enough, appeared to be a wind-driven dry nor'easter in South Jersey. The further north the storm traveled, the more devastating was its impact as it unleashed its fury battering sections of New England and the North Atlantic sweeping houses into the ocean and taking the lives of the Andrea Gail crew, setting the stage and providing the content for Sebastian Junger's creative genius leading to his captivating novel, *The Perfect Storm*.

Besides thunder and lightning and cyclonic storms, I also have a penchant for good old-fashioned snowstorms. Back in Chapter 3 of this memoir I cited the 1947 blizzard which occurred the day after Christmas when I was living in Port Republic, New Jersey. Grandpa Tucker Craig's tales of the famed Blizzard of 1888 and Mother Brown's excitement whenever it snowed fed my appetite and anticipation for snow. The 1950's produced several remarkable snowstorms, particularly the one in 1957 when my niece Dottie was a baby. That storm created drifts several feet high closing down Columbia Road in Nesco and opening the door to my first skiing adventure.

Somewhere in a storeroom or in a barn I had found a pair of skis. Lucky for me, a house was being built down the street near the church in Nesco, and workmen had left a mountain of earth perfect for my skiing adventure. Living in South Jersey, not known for ski trails or ski lifts but rather for mostly flatland, I set out all bundled up. Carrying my newly found skis, I trudged through snow drifts to reach my personal Mount Jack Frost. I can't quite remember how I attached the skis to my feet, but I did. I struggled to get myself to the top of the mountain. Gloves on my hands and skis on my feet, I stood surveying the winter landscape below. It turned out that I wasn't quite as agile as I had hoped to be. As I started down the mountain, I couldn't quite maneuver the downhill run that I pictured in my mind as the skis seemed awkwardly long and unwilling to cooperate, forcing me to roll down the mountain losing my skis before I was consumed by a huge snowdrift below.

Years later I would once again try skiing in Vermont in the late 1960's; I was about as successful then as I had been in my first ski launch. It was time for me to hang up my skis!

In 1978, Maria and I were in Florida at Disney when a full-blown blizzard crippled Atlantic City where Maria and I were living with her mother Jennie. The cancellation of air flights resulted in an extended vacation and a twenty-four hour Amtrak ride from Kissimmee, Florida, back to New Jersey. I really missed not being in the middle of that February blizzard.

You'll recall my falling asleep in a bathtub while reading Whittier's **Snowbound.** Several other literary snow adventures have kept me awake over the years, including Conrad Aiken's extraordinary short story, "Silent Snow, Secret Snow," Nathaniel Hawthorne's reality versus illusion story, "The Snow Image," and, of course, Chris Van Allsburg's amazing "The Polar Express" made into a film with the same title. Maria and I watch that film every Christmas, along with Alistair Sims' brilliant performance as Ebenezer Scrooge in Charles Dickens' *A Christmas Carol.*

The ecstatic joy that Ebenezer Scrooge expresses upon awakening from his ventures with the Ghosts of Christmas Past, Present, and Future mirrors the delight that I felt in the 1980's following an ice storm that transformed southern New Jersey's landscape into a crystalline wonderland. Linda Brennenstuhl, one of my high school students, captured the beauty of that extraordinary weather event in poetry:

I WOKE JUST IN TIME TO SEE MY WORLD AN
ICE FACTORY

My window seemed tangled
Flowers posing this way or that
The tree limbs just sort of dangled
On the line froze a red flannel hat.
Walking outside near the street
 Weeds stood formal and starched
 Unable to bow at my feet
They merely shivered and arched.

 Whoever heard of a glass roadway
 With icicle stop signs to warn
 A person to linger slow on this day
Taking it easy until days grow warm.
If I woke before daylight
 Perhaps I would have seen
The Mighty Gaffer, His blowpipe
 Poised above a glass-blown tree.

What beautiful imagery from a sixteen year old with a golden voice. That voice evokes another individual with a voice of gold, an individual whose name I gave to a stately Goldenrod plant in a 1989 "end of summer" piece which perfectly concludes this chapter.

GOLDENROD

My weatherman died just as summer ended this year, marking a tragic change in the forecast. A lover of life, Jim O'Brien: chrome-pony rider, telethon emcee, parade master, news anchorman and meteorologist who chose skydiving for his final performance as an unexpected twist of parachute lines entangled his life, climaxing in the death of this man for all seasons, just as summer turned to fall.

Oh, how he loved the exhilaration of the skydive! Just last week he had commented about the beauty of the sky and the sport as Chopper Six projected a panoramic view of the sun setting over Philadelphia during one of his forecasts. Oh, those forecasts, his Accu-Weather forecasts were a must. I'd even rush from the dinner table to hear about the bad guys and good guys, the highs and the lows, the record temperatures, and the bits of Americana in his own Yankee-Southern wit. Glued to the tube, I waited for his extended forecast, his apologies for Accu-Weather's inaccuracy, and his closing weather quips, such as "Glum." The weather arena was his territory, and the glummest outlook was so often mollified by O'Brien's good humor and hearty smile.

Glum—that sums up the forecast now that he is gone. Glum—that aptly describes the faces of a bereaved Jim Gardner, Don Tollefson, and other members of the Action Six News team struggling coura-geously to talk about the loss of a man who never appeared grim or glum; for his face and spirit sparkled as the lights and camera framed him at six and eleven o'clock for millions of viewers in the Delaware Valley.

I've heard crickets; I've seen stray monarchs and dying plants in the last few days, heralding the end of summer. In my backyard is a single, stately piece of goldenrod. That beautiful weed I've named Jim, for its golden hue and lankiness remind me of the transported Texan who could transform a piece of news or a weather report into something golden. Golden is the color of the sun, the color of the sky at times, the color of singularly cherished memories, the color that leaves are ready to assume, the color of life at its finest moments, the color that shines in wedding bands and jewels, the color of monarchs and their thrones, the color that transforms a season of green to one of majesty and glory. GOLDEN is Jim O'Brien, a composite of all that is golden delicious in what we have come to know in this life.

I wouldn't be surprised if Jim has been assigned a golden scepter to forecast the conditions of the universe in a realm far distant from earth. With that in mind, I'm planning to position my telescope to scan the skies to catch one of Jim's heavenly forecasts. It is bound to read: "And for tonight, folks, it looks like meteor showers and divine thunder—by the way, Gardner and Tollefson, where are all the bad guys?"

Yes, my weatherman died just as summer ended this year, marking a change in the extended forecast. Summer is over; it has taken with it a monument of a man whose very nature taught us to laugh, to live, and to love life. Such legacies can only color our lives golden, for in Jim O'Brien's passing we realize that we have been touched by a kind of Midas whose golden memory and zest for life will linger long after this summer, and the next, and the next.

I sent my tribute to Jim O'Brien to WPVI TV, Action 6 Channel News and received the following response from News Anchor, Jim Gardner.

WPVI TV

6

WPVI TV 4100 City Line Avenue
Philadelphia, Pennsylvania 19131
(215) 878-9700
Capital Cities Communications, Inc.

On behalf of the entire Channel 6 family and the
family of the late Jim O'Brien, we want you to
know how much we appreciated your expressions of
concern and sympathy. Be assured your message of
condolence will be forwarded to Jim's family in
Houston.

Sincerely,

Jim Gardner
ACTION NEWS

(23)

CHRISTMAS MEMORIES

I can still hear the bell. Can you? Christmas, a holiday unlike any other, celebrated in song, scripture, the arts, film and literature. One song calls it "the most wonderful time of the year." A familiar carol takes us on the journey of three kings from the Orient following "a star of wonder, star of night, star of royal beauty bright." Another carol, recently celebrating its two hundredth anniversary, colors that night silent and holy. The memory of my sister Margie singing "O Holy Night" in church, is Christmas, as are the memories of lighted candles, choir robes, and Carolyn Stewart playing an old pump organ as we sang "O Little Town of Bethlehem," "Hark the Herald Angels Sing," and "Joy to the World."

Mother Brown's soprano voice still echoes in my mind as the spirit of Christmases past flickers in the candles at the New Columbia Methodist Church, candles that Maria and I donated in Mother Brown's memory after she passed in 1993.

Our first Christmas with the Browns in 1949 was special; it was really the first Christmas that I recall with any clarity. We all helped decorate the Christmas tree before we three kids were sent up to wooden hill in anticipation of Santa's arrival. I remember laughing the first time Mother told us it was time for Wooden Hill. That first Christmas Eve I was both excited and restless, and at one point I got off the "hill" just in time to catch a glimpse of Santa (Father Brown) about to descend the hallway staircase with a wooden sled for us kids. Merry Christmas!

There were other presents that Christmas: colorfully embroidered cowboy shirts for Victor and me from Aunt Ada Bradley, mother's cousin, a slinky for Victor and a doctor's kit for me. Father's sister, Bunny Tramutola, who was very creative, molded a ceramic mug with an elephant and the name Danny with the year 1949 etched on its base. I still have that mug. I remember Margie getting a baton and a guitar which I am sure opened the door to her love for country music, and later on in her life, for Elvis Presley. There would be other Christmases, but the memories of that first one with my foster parents, the Browns, will linger forever.

Other Christmases brought other presents, ice skates and roller skates. It didn't take long for us to wear out the roller skates, skating up and down the macadam on Columbia Road. The ice skates, on the other hand, were more durable as we sharpened our blades, skills, and imaginations preparing for future Winter Olympics as we skated the night away on Aunt Hazel's and Uncle Leo's frozen pond in a wooded area off Moores Avenue. What cold fun we had!

Aunt Hazel was very much the spirit of Christmas and chose her gifts with loving care. To this day I treasure two very special gifts from her: a ceramic replica of Rodin's "The Thinker" and a black ribbon book marker with my three initials, DNW. One Christmas Eve she and I worked together wrapping packages and getting a tree for a little girl in our town who would not have had a Christmas if we had not provided one. That incident taught me the meaning of reaching out to someone less fortunate. The occurrence was the catalyst for a tender story that I wrote as a freshman at Glassboro State College and submitted to my creative writing teacher, Dr. Marie Campbell. The story was entitled "A Christmas for Gertrude." A short excerpt from the story sets the stage for what became an eventful night:

> Peering through the window I saw a scene which
> made me change my mind. There was no wreath
> on the door or at the windows. There was no tree
> in the corner. The little girl, Gertrude, sat on a
> stool wrapped in a blanket. Her mother sat in a chair

with a forlorn expression. As I turned from the scene,
I thought of something I had said earlier in the evening,
"There are a lot of children who may not enjoy one
Christmas a year."

That thought hastened my steps to my Aunt Hazel's house, and I told
her what I had seen upon looking through Gertrude's window. The two of
us literally created "A Christmas for Gertrude."

From the story:
Grandpa Tucker carried in the tree, Aunt Hazel, the gifts,
Grandmother Craig, the decorations, and I carried Uncle
Leo's gift, a turkey he had won in a raffle. Little Gertrude
danced around as we decorated the tree; Grandpa Tucker
got the woodstove burning. We all knew how happy we
were making this family.

Gertrude's story celebrates the joy of Christmas and giving. It
reminds me of that beautiful O'Henry story, "The Gift of the Magi," and
sacrifices made sealing the bond of love between Della and her husband.

Father Brown's Aunt Margaret and Uncle Morris Parker, who lived
in Atlantic City, were house guests at Christmas when father drove to
Atlantic City to get them. I can still taste the delicious raisin cookies from
Kent's Restaurant that they brought with them. Those cookies rivaled the
delicious dark ginger Johnny Cake with raisins that Mother Brown baked
every Christmas. Aunt Margaret and Uncle Morris were the special aunt
and uncle who bequeathed that rich collection of books to mother and
father. Curious that a volume of O'Henry's short stories was among that
collection of books. That was when I first read "The Gift of the Magi."

Decorating our old Colonial house and trimming the tree were
special times growing up in Nesco. I always looked forward to climbing
the winding staircase into the attic to retrieve the ornaments stored there.
Red cellophane lighted bubble wreaths were part of the ornament collection, along with a papier mache santa that mother said was over seven-
ty-five years old. And of course there were those ancient rusted sleigh bells

attached to a strip of leather which I could imagine ringing years ago on a horse and sleigh when the Old Union Hotel was in its heyday. I hung those bells on the screen of the brick fireplace in the living room where we decorated the tree with real tinsel and an angel at the top.

One Christmas I drove father's Chevy pick-up truck to Uncle Leo's to cut down a tree. Uncle Leo helped me with the chopping, and we loaded it into the truck. When I arrived back home, the tree was missing. I quickly retraced my steps, and, sure enough, I found the tree in the middle of Columbia Road where it had fallen off the truck. You'll remember that I worked with Uncle Leo in the summer collecting cattails. Well, in winter he collected evergreens and made wreaths and grave blankets. He used holly, pinecones and some of the dried bayberry to decorate his wreaths and grave blankets; Aunt Hazel used plastic red bows as a finishing touch for uncle's handiwork. They always gave us at least two wreaths which were used to decorate the two doors at the front of our historical Colonial home.

Mother Brown loved singing and never missed any of the Christmas concerts that I participated in while in high school and Glassboro State College. At Glassboro, the girls' dorms were decorated and competed with one another for prizes. When mother came to the college, I took her on a tour to see those decorations. Looking back, I realize how many miles she traveled all by herself to attend those concerts. What a special lady she was in my life.

During my courtship of Maria Victoria Anna Di Giovanni, my bride-to-be, I planned a way to surprise her with an engagement ring at Christmas by sealing the ring in a tiny red porcelain santa to which I added a piece of orange cord. As we decorated the tree in 1963, I hung the tiny santa on a branch at her home on 4 North Montpelier Avenue in Atlantic City. Naturally, I purposely directed her attention to the hanging Santa, and she was surprised when she discovered what the Santa contained. That little Santa is most often the first decoration to be placed on the tree each year. This past Christmas, 2019, marked the fifty-fifth time that we hung that little porcelain guy on the tree.

Our Christmas tree has always been a work of art. Maria recalls the year that her brother Paul was home to decorate the tree, and since he didn't find the tree full enough, he drilled holes into the tree, adding limbs. Maria also tells the story of the year that Paul decided to spray the tree with fake snow. Unfortunately, he sprayed it with all of the ornaments on the tree. To this day, some of those ornaments remain a part of our collection. Besides that little santa, we have a balsam angel with a long history that sits atop the tree, along with a collection of antique ornaments, including a set of glass bells in blue, red and amber, and a tiny pearlized one that usually hangs from the angel's hand; it is the oldest ornament on the tree. Over the years, our ornament collection has grown and includes assorted Christopher Radko ornaments, hand-made originals from the local Charity League, Olive tree ornaments from Bethlehem, glass-blown items from Europe, a collection of starched, hand-crocheted shoes which our friend Joe Tozzi places on the tree each year, winged angels from France, and a rich collection of special novelty ornaments acquired from friends and family over the years.

Our Christmases at 4 North Montpelier were truly memorable. Maria's brother Paul usually came home to celebrate with us. His gifts were always exceptional: recordings by Elisabeth Schwarzkopf, Leontyne Price, Joan Baez and other artists, including a copy of his own Sideshow album recording in 1970. For Maria and her mother there were beautiful scarves, an exquisite robe, an embroidered silk shawl, and a dress from one of the shops in New York's Greenwich Village. The year Peter Shaffer came to dinner, he presented us with a magnificent numbered pen and ink etching featuring a bearded immigrant with a baby resting its head on his shoulder. The etching reminds Maria of her father who, at seventeen, made his way to America in 1913 from Macchia D'Isernia, Italy, with his brother Loreto aboard the Napoli. That etching is still with us, hanging in our living room.

Holiday meals were a core part of Christmas at the Di Giovanni household and included the traditional seven fishes on Christmas Eve, and a host of tantalizing pasta dishes with homemade sauce, meatballs, sausage, braciole, and pasta with garlic and oil (aglio e olio) with anchovies. And, of course, there were delicious homemade butter cookies, including that holiday favorite, cioffe, prepared by Aunt Millie Di Giovanni, Mother Jennie, and my sweet Maria. We had fruitcake, chocolates from Jagielky's and all sorts of pies, including my hands-down favorite, mincemeat, for which Maria is the master baker. Sometimes, mincemeat pie is served at both Thanksgiving and Christmas! Hallelujah! Lastly, I cannot overlook Aunt Theresa Sanderlin's Italian cheese cake, Aunt Anna Acciavatti's larger than life strawberry shortcake, Aunt Rose Kelly's zucchini quiche, and Aunt Marian Martino's Jeanettes. Specialties like those from my new-found Italian relatives awakened tastebuds I never knew I had!

In the breakfront in our living room are stored two very special items that are brought out only at Christmas. One is an 1896 copy of Clement Moore's *The Night Before Christmas or A Visit of St Nicholas*, published by McLaughlin Brothers in New York. I often placed it in a showcase for students and faculty to see. Surprised I was when our school's Media Department asked me to do a taped reading of the beloved story which became an annual event broadcast through 'Gami TV throughout the school. The best part was that the colorful illustrations from my 1896 copy, now a hundred and twenty-four years old, were used to accompany my reading which I presented wearing a Santa cap.

The other precious item housed in the china closet is a relatively new copy of Charles Dickens' *A Christmas Carol*. What makes the edition special is the signature on the title cover page: Cedric Charles Dickens, the great, great, grandson of the famous English author. I met Cedric at an English conference in 1986 and purchased the copy of my all-time favorite Christmas story which Cedric Charles Dickens autographed. I can't imagine a Christmas without reading or seeing some version of *A Christmas Carol* in the same way that I cannot imagine Christmas without holly, especially holly with bright red berries.

I'm not sure when my fixation with holly began, but it was long before I married Maria in 1964. I vividly recall treks into the woods behind our home in Nesco. I loved those woods, deep, dark woods. It was in those woods that I first found uncultivated holly trees, some with berries and some without. Somewhere I read about the legend of the holly believed to be a sacred plant with magical powers, believed to bring good luck and protection into one's house. Perhaps that is why I began cutting holly back in the 1950's and taking it into the house, filling vases and decorating with it. I don't recall telling my brother Victor about the special powers or the good luck attributed to the holly plant, but I do remember getting a cursing out from him one year when he reacted to the prickly holly leaves that ended up in his bed from the holly branches I had used to decorate our bedroom. For years, I have gathered holly branches as part of our Christmas décor. For a number of years, Joe Tozzi, a good friend, aware of my love for holly, has secretly located sources of beautiful berried holly which he clips and loads into his truck and delivers to our garage or alleyway. Joe had a stroke in December, 2018, one day before his birthday. About a week and a half before his stroke, he arrived at our house in Margate with a load of the prettiest holly I have seen in years!

Another friend of Maria's and mine is Clement Wasleski whom one might take for Saint Nicholas himself during the Christmas season as he grows a beard every year and wears a Santa outfit in the days leading up to and after Christmas. He truly loves preparing and decorating for the holidays. His Christmas tree and home are magnificently decorated and, invariably, he or his wife Faye will call in mid-December to see if we want any of the branches he has trimmed from his live tree. Of course I accept the offer, for I will use those branches, along with holly and other trimmings, to create original grave blankets for family members who have passed on over the years.

For all of our married life, Maria and I have traveled hundreds of miles at Christmastime transporting gifts to our relatives in Nesco, Hammonton, and Folsom. At the same time, we have transported beautifully decorated grave blankets for the cemeteries in Pleasant Mills, Hammonton, Pleasantville, and Mays Landing, New Jersey. Those grave blankets are made with love and respect for all of the following deceased family members: Dorothy and William Brown, Louisa and Thomas Craig, Hazel and Leo Landy, Victor and Phyllis Walters, Marguerite Craig, Jennie and Paul DiGiovanni, Paul Giovanni, Angelina and Nunzio Martino, Carmella and Loreto Di Giovanni, Victoria and Domenick Formica, Rose and James

Kelly, Theresa and George Sanderlin, Anna and Ettore Acciavatti, Marian and Peter Martino, and as of Christmas 2019, a special arrangement for someone who was very much a family member, the gatherer of holly, Joseph P. Tozzi who passed away in October, 2019.

Joe Tozzi, the Holly Gatherer

All of those relatives are family, the saints and poets whom I have met and loved over the course of my journey from Baltimore so many years ago. They are central to my journey, and as many of them passed from this life to the next, I felt a calling to honor them, to eulogize them. And so, the next segment of this memoir is an extended celebration, through personally written and presented eulogies of those who while living, both family and friends, gave me unconditional love during a journey that has advanced an awkward little boy and ward of the state to an accomplished and grateful adult.

IN MEMORIAM: A GALLERY OF EULOGIES

Dorothy Ada Brown.....March 10, 1910-June 15, 1993

June is busting out all over; it's in the magnolias Aunt Hazel picked near the old iron bridge on the fifteenth, the day mother passed away. June…it's the anniversary of Margie's and my Nesco arrival on the thirteenth of June, forty-four years ago. June--Dottie's and Kermit's thirteenth wedding anniversary on the eighth of June. June--the sixty-third wedding anniversary of Mother and Father Brown. June sixth when we were all last together. My birthday on the nineteenth and Maria's and my wedding anniversary on the twentieth.

June…who could forget Aunt Hazel's, Hilda's and Carolyn's and Alton's birthdays? June, June, June is busting out all over!

I'm taking you back, back with me to memories of Dear Dorothy in a month pregnant with living and dying and busting out all over…

Strawberry and blueberry patches and picking berries in season busting out all over…Harvesting dreams and memories of mother's soprano singing "In The Garden" at the New Columbia United where I can hear Reverend Ebel preaching and bees buzzing if you're listening to Grandpa Tucker shouting and sweet Louisa smiling while Uncle Leo's cutting cattails on a day like today with Pat Boone writing love letters in the sand as mother ironed June shirts and shorts in the t.v. room where June nights echoed "Your Hit parade," "Our Miss Brooks," "Ed Sullivan Show," "Amos and Andy," "Hawkins Falls," and "One Man's Family."

With all those beginnings and endings in June, perhaps June is Janus looking back and looking forward to all the years it took us to get this far to revel in the memory of Mother Brown, the Old Union Hotel, and Joe Mulliner.

Dear Dorothy whose child-like presence created a yellow brick road for her children, grandchildren and great grandchildren.

Mother whose rich imagination and maternal instincts fashioned a home for us, dried our tears, baked us biscuits and strawberry shortcakes, helped us with our lessons, taught us right from wrong, celebrated our birthdays and holidays, encouraged, scolded, took pride in our accomplishments and just plain loved Donald and Franny and Victor and Teeny and Martha and Eric and Jason and Victor and Donna and Victor and Kim and Katie and Christopher and Kermit and Andy and Brandy and Steven and Timmy and Margie and Dottie and Maria and Hazel and Therese and Leo and Bill… June…June…June is busting out all over and Nesco's abuzz with the news eternal. God bless her soul.

William Henry Brown……July 10, 1906-April 7, 1995

I am going back in time to June, 1949, to a warm summer's day when Uncle Bill and Aunt Dot opened the doors of the Old Union Hotel with their hearts and arms to welcome Margie and me, and later, our brother Victor, giving us a place to live. Several months would pass before we gained enough trust to call Aunt Dot and Uncle Bill, Mother and Father, but we did, and today marks the end of an era; for father's passing forces me to pick up his magnifying glass and try to bring into focus the courage, strength and magnanimity of a simple and elusive man who accepted a huge responsibility and significantly changed our lives.

In our growing up, father was tall; his was a tall quiet strength marked by duty to work and family. Someone must have warned him about the illness of idleness, for he always seemed busy, tinkering, plowing a field, looking for a grub hoe, riding a lawnmower, driving a well, planting corn, building a corn crib, slaughtering a hog, picking strawberries (eating more than went into the quart box, resulting in mother's boxing his ears)—oh how William worked, and I think he liked work, for I remember his whistling while he worked.

His work also transported him to Philadelphia as an electrician at Disston's; we never talked much about his work there, but his magnifying glass and my memory bring into focus an important connection: he loved carting things, not just field corn for the pigs, but other things, like saw handles which he burned in the woodstove, and big, heavy grindstones, and best of all those granite rocks that he carted home and piled in the backyard. I couldn't imagine what they were for, and I don't think he could either, but all that hard work and lifting had to lead to something. And you know what? That pile of granite rocks became a bridge for my imagination, a mountain of metaphors for reaching beyond the ordinary, everyday and humdrum—my own Mount Palomar smack in the middle of the universe in Bill Brown's backyard just because he loved carting things. Why I'd been to the top before Martin Luther King ever made his speech, thanks to Bill Brown.

Those rocks held some other lessons for father, also, for in recent years and days he managed, daily, to muster a granite-like strength as he moved a mountain every day, lifting himself from bed to wheelchair, transforming himself through indomitable will and enviable courage into a herculean figure who scaled Mount Everest every day he lived. Oh, what lessons of life he taught us!

And you know what? Through all that daily struggle he always managed to smile, to see humor in things; he made us laugh more than he made us cry. The day before he died we laughed about his favorite television show, "In the Heat of the Night." And on the day he died, he recounted with steel-trap clarity his 1936 appendectomy and the fury of the great hurricane of 1944. The Old Union Hotel almost lost a tree in that hurricane, and in the most recent storm has lost a generational resident. Our father's passing marks the end of a significant era, for with mother he provided a foundation for all of us through all the years of our lives, and for all the generations to follow.

What an extraordinary human being whom we honor and remember today in so many different ways: husband, master electrician, volunteer fireman and fire chief, local humorist, bridge builder, mountain climber, brother, uncle, grandpop, pop, father, daddy and, one final epithet, the Birdman of the Old Union Hotel. How he loved the birds and loved feeding them. And, if you use your imagination for a moment, you might transform the Old Union Hotel into a nesting place where a group of starlings with broken wings were invited in, cared for, fed, healed, loved and readied for their next journeys. For Father Brown, the Birdman of the Old Union Hotel, this life's journey has ended, and like one of the birds he helped to nurture, he has taken flight this time, leaving behind a rich legacy as he soars freer and higher than he has ever flown before. Rest in peace.

Hazel Craig Landy.....June 4, 1920-April 26, 1995

Recently, I was looking through my Bible and came across a floral cross. On the back, in ink, was the message, "Happy Easter, Dan, Love, Aunt Hazel, March 29, 1959. By 1959, I had been in Nesco for almost ten years and had grown to love my outspoken and sometimes shocking Aunt Hazel who wasted no time in telling you off if you deserved it—or if you didn't! She waged an argument with the dexterity of a barracuda—according to her husband, my Uncle Leo--- and generally kept the town astir and informed by telephone or any other means. Able to talk for hours at a time without saying anything—according to her late husband, my Uncle Leo, who wasn't always right.

Not only did she love the news, she was the news, and newsworthy. She was stylish, up to the minute, always in fashion. Most recently, she had her picture taken with Bishop Neil Irons, and as our church historian, on the day she died she entertained the ladies from the Ocean County Historical Society, giving them a history of Nesco—one I am sure they will never forget!

Kermit said to me not long ago, "What will we do after Aunt Hazel is gone? She's one of the last of an era." Well, Kermit, we waited just a little too long, and she has left us breathless, shocked, and sad.

As far as history, I will always cherish memories of growing up and being made to feel a part of the Landy family with Aunt Hazel's ability to make you feel and believe that you were special. Everyone of us sitting here today experienced some significant moment in time that made us feel better because of Aunt Hazel's love, generosity, and deep-down caring. When we were growing up, she never forgot a birthday. And her special gifts, like "The Thinker" figurine and the bookmark with my initials reflected the meticulous care and time she took in selecting something special that connected us in time forever, a tie that binds. All of us here today have such recollections which flash upon the inward eye—like Wordsworth's daffodils—which is the bliss of solitude, the tie that binds each of us to the memory and presence of the late great Hazel Craig Landy.

She was the spirit of Christmas. She was the wife of a prisoner of war. They named a hurricane after her in 1954. She was Mable to Uncle Leo; she was mother to Leo Junior and Therese, sister to Becky, Dot and Alton, Grandmother to George, Triddle, Melissa, Leo III and Jack, and Great Grandmother to their children. She worried about all of those she loved and willingly sacrificed for them. To a large population she was adopted as Aunt Hazel. A curly white-haired beautiful woman in her later years, someone who was forever young, someone whose energy, humor, wit, inquisitiveness, charity, willingness to march for a cause, endless stories and zest for life made life so much richer!

What will we do after Aunt Hazel has gone? The moment is here. We will pause in respect. We will adorn her with lilacs and heather, purple irises, and roses, and a garland of cats paws and cattails woven together with love and dried flowers and grasses from the fields. We might even recommend to Mayor Ramp that June fourth, her birthday, be declared a special day of remembrance. And finally, in our sorrow we will weep here at her graveside. And, at some unexpected moment when a memory or thought of her flashes upon the inward eye, I will remember that little cross she gave me with the Happy Easter message. On the front of it, below the flowers, is a line from Matthew 28:20; it reads, "…Lo, I am with you always…" In truth, the spirit of Hazel Craig Landy will be with us always.

Ralph W. Martin…..July 19, 1931- May 19, 1997

> "When lilacs last in the dooryard bloomed
> And the great star droop'd in the western sky in the night.
> I mourn'd, and yet shall mourn with ever returning spring,
> Ever returning spring, trinity sure to me you bring
> Lilac blooming perennial and drooping star in the west…"
> (Walt Whitman)

And thoughts of Ralph W. Martin, always a smile, always a gentleman, shrewd, focused, counselor, bookkeeper of the accounts. Human. In touch. Always glad to see you. Distinguished me from the other Dan Walters by my middle initial "N" which he declared stood for "Nut." Sometimes months would pass before we saw one another; yet, it was always as if we had never been apart. He made you feel that you counted; he made you feel comfortable. He exuded pride in himself and his daily work; he was forever young, vital and tuned to a world that he vigorously demanded to be a part of, and a world to which he helped bring order. In my last face-to-face encounter with him at that now historic 12/5 meeting, I shook his hand and praised him for an extraordinary performance after which he said, "You were my mentor." In truth, he was mine and that of many seated here today. What humility, what a model citizen, what a tireless worker. What an eternal friend to us, to the district, to education. God rest his soul as he seeks higher ground and eternal rest as all of us, in our grief, realize that his vacant chair can never be filled as we remember in "…ever-returning Spring, trinity sure to us you bring Lilac blooming perennial and drooping star in the west…"

And thoughts of Ralph W. Martin

Rose M. Kelly…..March 21, 1909-September 21, 2001

My Dear Aunt Rose,

The Lariope in our garden has never been more beautiful, and Henry Fonda, a beautiful yellow-faced rose, the last one of summer, is in full bloom as I write this to you. Both the Lariope and that beautiful rose remind me of your sunshine, wisdom and love. It saddens me that you are gone, but I am happy, in a way, because the recent days of turmoil in our country have left all of us somewhat numb. I wrote about those images of September 11 just about the same time that you decided to take your leave, and then I decided to dedicate my poem entitled "Without License" to you, your memory, and the memory of all those patriots who died.

WITHOUT LICENSE

Without a rally or calling of troops
We went to war last Tuesday
Without a warning, heart or conscience
A clandestine enemy invaded American soil
As superpower technology televised the events
To numbed viewers dazed by yet another
Shot heard 'round the world.
Aftershocks compounded the nightmare
And horror howled, "My God America is bleeding"
From an offensive attack by hijacked planes
Trespassing, bombing, terrifying
New York, Washington and Pennsylvania airways
Worldtrade Pentagon hijacked passengers

Rerouted and forced to face senseless, untimely deaths
In twin towering infernos and a ruptured Pentagon
Consumed by explosions and implosions of heat and hate
Collapsing buildings burying hopes of humans alive
Destroying edifices and occupants who
Stood freely only seconds before the attack
Singing and drinking coffee in the midst of
Good morning, America.

Somber songs now sweep the nation
Weeping and wailing patriotic melodies
For the living and the dead
There is work to be done and calls to be answered
My country 'tis of thee
Oh beautiful for spacious skies
God bless America
And that distant heart-broken good-bye
 From a doomed cell phone caller.

And in our grief we call upon God's blessing for the late great
Rose Kelly, loving mother, sister, grandmother, great-grandmother, cousin, aunt, patriot, humanitarian, humorist, and
the maker of the best zucchini quiche in the world!

Eugene Compton....December 2, 1936-May 9, 2002

It isn't easy to find the words to console those who have lost
a husband, father, grandfather, brother, nephew, cousin,
colleague, or friend. Gene Compton, teacher extraordinaire,
educational supervisor, city councilman, and community
activist held so many titles and earned so many awards that
we are left breathless and in awe of his accomplishments.
And, he was always so humble about his accomplishments,
preparing, it seemed, for the next venture.

Everyone will mourn something in his absence because his presence lit up a room, and he always had something to say—something witty, thoughtful, or just downright funny. I'll miss those special pictures he was always taking or finding somewhere: a snapshot of a family member, a friend, a picture of him with a celebrity, or out on a boat, or a picture of a sunset, an enormous apple, or some other extraordinary image that he just had to share. My, how he loved life!

I just loved Gene's practical and aesthetic sense; he could fix almost anything, and he zipped through computer operations, always ready to help those of us who were not quite as computer-literate. How much I learned from him, and his help always came with that smile—that wonderful smile.

He really was an extraordinary educator. I always saw him as someone on the cutting edge, and Dona Stepp and I would often kid him about where his next trip or conference would take him. He always came back excited about some new idea or direction. He was always interested in that blending of image and art resulting in an original graphic, design, concept or idea. In so many ways he helped his students, colleagues, and community look beyond the moment. He helped to shape the future.

Donna Stepp and I had a special relationship with Gene. We three adults had formed a friendship pact and called ourselves the Three Musketeers. I am sure that in our hearts and minds' eye that special relationship will remain intact as we mourn his passing, remembering, always, Gene's zest for life, his love for family and friends, his creative spirit, his laughter, his Jim Backus impression, all of his special gifts, and the indelible memory that is so uniquely GENE COMPTON. God rest his soul.

Marc Lee Rosenberg.....February 9, 1956-July 31, 2008

STILL LIFE

Good fences make good neighbors. Marc and I shared a
common fence, Monmouth Avenue, and we often crossed
over to settle the matters of the world, to chat about his work
and family, or to examine the goings-on in my garden. One
day this past spring I invited him over to see the peonies that
had finally bloomed after a long trial of planting, replanting,
and finding just the right conditions for them to bloom. I was
moved by Marc's interest in those peonies, his enthusiasm for
life, and other garden conversations that revealed his deep
concern for humanity and the human condition. I promised to let him know when Mr. Lincoln, a beautiful red rose
variety, was in bloom. Our over the fence chats were little
slices of life now ingrained in my mind forever, much like
the images in a still life. Robert Creely's "Dried Roses" echoes
my sentiments in his line from that poem, "the wonders we
thought to remember." ***The wonders we thought to remember***—Marc Rosenberg was such a wonder, and I dedicate this
original poem to him and his memory:

GATHERING LILACS

Yesterday was the day to gather lilac
Blossoms of violet with heart-shaped leaves
Intoxicating scents of Whitman's imagery
When last they bloomed in the dooryard,
My connection with those Civil War blossoms
Of redolent nectar scent without equal;
Lilac laced memory is a time tunnel
With a scent so profound that it rivals
The aromatic perfume of Whitman's lilacs

Discovered while foraging amidst Leaves of
Grass in a distant classroom
Lilacs
Weeping at Lincoln's doorstep
Lilacs
Announcing the end of the Civil War,
The loss of America's innocence,
The death of a President
Draped in noble deep purple of lilac hue—
Yesterday was the day I gathered
Lilacs

A backdrop for all of our lives…A Still Life…And the wonders we will always remember: Abraham Lincoln freeing the slaves; Michelangelo freeing The David and The Prisoners through sculpted marble; and, Marc Rosenberg creating and freeing majestic images of light and beauty as precious as springtime peonies forever captured in a spectacular glass still life.

Anna Rita Acciavatti…..September 27, 1913-January 18, 2011

A beautiful lady, Anna Rita Martino Acciavatti was so many things to so many people. Her niece Maria, my wife, said that she would want to thank her for the memories: Memories of the downbeach Sister Act featuring Aunt Rose, Aunt Anna, and Aunt Theresa. Memories of family gatherings, cooking and baking, Uncle Ettore and his wine cellar. All of those beautiful children, grandchildren, and great-grandchildren and all of their pictures attached to the refrigerator door. Working on the Boardwalk…Sister Jennie, Giovanni's, Jewels Of The World. Feeding the throngs at Margate Terrace, all that living and tending to. All of that aluminum foil around the oven door on Arctic Avenue. And for me, in particular, those home-made cinnamon buns, giant chocolate chip cookies, pound cake, and, of course, that three-story high strawberry shortcake—oh, my, Aunt Anna, what a memory! When I retired five years ago, you sent me a card and wrote, "Dear nephew, God loves you and so do I."

Dear, dear Aunt Anna, Mom Mom, you are now with God, and all of us will always love you and remember the joy you brought to our lives. Bless you, Aunt Anna.

Theresa Martino Sanderlin.....November 24, 1918 - May 25, 2012

What's new that's not old? Sound familiar? If you ask that question, you must remember to have one hand on your hip and a beautiful smile on your face. Unforgettable Aunt Theresa. Unforgettable, too, were those endless cheesecakes, and those individually wrapped slices of pound cake, and that chicken soup with all those vegetables, and, of course, those panettones from Shop Rite. Theresa Sanderlin was living theatre and told great stories. She not only told the story but like her brother Pete she would get up and act it out. She should have been given a Tony or Emmy Award—certainly an award for life-time achievement. Achievements? Raising a family. Living with arthritis her entire life but always keeping those fingers and hands busy working in a factory, as a sales lady extraordinaire at Giovanni's, baking pound cakes for her son's business, making ham pie at Easter, learning to drive when she was in her fifties, and preparing treats for all of those residents at Margate Terrace. She mastered Spanish to the point where she preferred the Spanish channel to any other. She grew basil beneath a crocheted lampshade she had created; and, of course, she maintained a lifetime of devotion to the Blessed Mother. We all knew how many years she lived in Margate Terrace and that at ninety-four she was the oldest resident whose daily walks up and down those hallways emulated some of the best athletes on any team. And then, of course, there was the time she fell and broke her shoulder and informed the doctor that it would be too hot for her to travel for therapy. She asked the doctor what therapy and exercises were needed and managed to heal herself at home. She even gave me a demonstration of what to do after I broke my shoulder. What a remarkable woman she was who deeply loved her family: her three Georges, sisters and brothers, nieces and nephews, grandchildren and great grandchildren. What's new that's not old?—Dear Theresa Martino Sanderlin was forever new, never old. How we loved her, and how certain we are that she and her sisters Mary, Jennie, Rose, and Anna are reunited in Heaven continuing any unfinished arguments begun while here on earth.

Our lives will be very different without Dear Aunt Theresa. The last of a great generation, she will be missed at ShopRite on Thursday mornings; she will be missed by that gentleman who brought her communion whom she gave a five dollar bill, and most of all, she will be missed by all of us here today. May she rest in peace.

Victoria Di Giovanni Formica......November 8, 1917-August 17, 2013

Victoria—what a beautiful name, from the Latin meaning victory, conqueror, triumphant. We gather today to honor the memory and victories of our Victoria: mother, sister, aunt, grandmother, great-grandmother, god-mother, and special cousin.

Victoria really is a beautiful name, and I came to realize its power when Maria and I traveled to Macchia D'Isernia where Victoria's father Loreto was born. The excitement of that

Italian journey was punctuated by an outburst at the home of a new-found cousin with whom we shared family photographs from America. It was a picture of Victoria that caused a stir. Someone went running to find a picture of Esterina whom Victoria greatly resembled. Esterina was one of her father's sisters. Victoria was named after her grandmother Victoria, Loreto and Paolo DiGiovanni's mother.

Victoria—what a beautiful name transported from one continent to another as were the immigrant journeys of the Di Giovannis and Formicas united in love, marriage and family ties. Dear Victoria Di Giovanni Formica—how she loved family and family gatherings—all of those parties and memories and food—all of those special occasions at Café 2825, Touch of Italy, Sage and, of course, at 107 North Montpelier Avenue. Dear Victoria, what a triumphant, long-lived journey she has made: successful business woman working side-by-side with her dear husband Domenick, wife, mother, community activist, a long-standing parishioner of St. Michael's, and a matriarch binding the lives and loves of her brother Charles, his wife Mary and their children: Larry, Ronnie, and Maria; and, her own children: Charles, Harry and Loretta; her grandchildren: Michael, James, Dominick, Bob and Jennifer, her precious great-grand-daughter, Isabella, and her god-child, Maria Victoria DiGiovanni Walters.

Victoria has truly come full circle. Her beautiful smile, regal presence, love of life and family have brought her to this victorious moment passing from this life to the triumphant gates of Heaven. God rest Victoria.

Angelo Stoicos…..July 15,1929- December 28, 2013

A memorable line from the famous English play, **Charley's Aunt**, occurs when someone turns to Donna Lucia

D'Alvadorez, who is from Brazil where the nuts come from, and says, "You are an enigma, a puzzle." What a perfect description for our dearly departed Angelo who was an enigma, a puzzle. I couldn't find that characteristic when researching *Stoicos* (though "stoic" he was), or Evangelos, his actual first name which translates from the Greek as the "good news messenger." Angelo was a complex person, for sure, with a quick wit and a good sense of humor. I often suggested that he write a book and fill it with his great one-liners. He was naturally funny. Having him arrive to repair a burglar alarm could be an alarming experience in itself. Sometimes the alarm never got repaired as he found a comfortable chair and waxed on about life and eating the right things while drinking cup after cup of coffee. His opening greeting might well have been, "So what's your incapacitation?" which might have been nothing more than a needed repair with a phillips screwdriver.

How he loved his okra and leeks. How he complained about oranges and bananas which no longer had any taste. My wife Maria and I lived through all his tirades as he condemned this food or that and then proceeded to ask for the salt shaker. He could talk to anybody and loved the beach and all of his Boardwalk cronies with whom he argued endlessly about who discovered America. Angelo was convinced that it was a Greek. He was proud of his Greek heritage and declared without reservation that he was a Macedonian and descendant of Alexander the Great. Maria was convinced that he kept a camel in his closet!

Lured by the wonder of it all, his curiosity was an enviable trait as he dug into old copies of National Geographic and history. He had the Midas touch when it came to fixing or repairing anything. He also had a special sensitivity and caring for older people. Like Mark Twain, he grew somewhat bitter and disillusioned in his later years finding it painful to lose so many friends with whom he had special attachments. Near the end of his life he became a living definition of the word "stoic" which was core to his surname, Stoicos. I can still see him fighting the wind riding his bike. There were times when he was so completely relaxed that Maria joked about getting a mirror to see if he was still breathing. Unruffled, his greatest strength was his ability to steadfastly follow his path, preferring to keep himself to himself believing that to be the best way to ensure a happy and stress-free existence.

Calm, thoughtful, cautious, and wary all describe Angelaluk, a special name I had for him. He loved Charley Chaplin; his favorite film was **City Lights**. Reminiscent of Chaplin in life, Angelo made us laugh and cry. As sunlight fades on his favorite city of lights, Atlantic City, we remember a remarkable man for whom we missed the chance—before today—to say good-bye. ANGELO STOICOS…God rest his soul.

*Angelo was the step-father of Dean Lipoff, a young man whom Maria and I nurtured through adolescence and beyond. He and his wife Sarah and their daughter Ivy live in San Anselmo, California. They are a very special extended family.

Marguerite M. Walters Craig…December 23, 1936-June 18, 2014

All shook up. And rightly so. We can hear her voice. We can see her Elvis costume and impersonation. We can see and hear her performing at Katie's and Brian's wedding and at the homestead in Nesco, Those are wonderful memories, along with picking blueberries and strawberries, and Margie's pig Petunia who won a blue ribbon at the 4-H fair.

Her great sense of humor kept us in stitches, and from the earliest days of our lives in Baltimore she was a big sister who looked after Victor and me.

We all know how much she loved us, for she never ended a phone conversation or a bedside visit without telling us how much she loved us. It has been a long journey from that long ago Palm Sunday train ride from Baltimore to Atlantic City destined to become wards of the state, living in a variety of foster homes, and finally realizing the true sense of the word "family" when the Browns of Nesco welcomed Margie, Victor and me into their home. They gave us a sense of security, religion, and some rules about right and wrong.

Margie was always a standout comedienne and an exceptional musical talent; she loved the drums and played that trumpet in the Hammonton High School Band and Orchestra; she strutted when she played.

Without question, the birth of her daughter Dorothy Virginia changed all of our lives, and Dottie has been the anchor for her mother throughout much of her life, and particularly in her final days.

I can't help but imagining Margie in Heaven tuning up her harp and leading a band of angels in a medley of Elvis hits. There is sunlight in the midst of our sorrow. At rest, her spirit calls to us to remember her, to love her, and always to love one another. I can hear her singing "Are You Lonesome Tonight?" And, yes, we will miss her; we will be lonesome without her, but comforted, perhaps, by that distant call of the whippor-will. Our spirits will rise remembering how she made us laugh, that she knew how to have a good time, that she was an exceptional vocalist and musician, that she is finally at peace, that she was able to live to see the birth of her great-grand-daughter, Kendall Jane.

Mother, sister, aunt, grandmother, great-grandmother, and loyal friend whose courageous strength and depth of love will nourish us in the days that lie ahead. Marguerite Madeline Walters Craig, Rest in Peace.

Post Script: Before my sister Margie died, doctors had performed a tracheotomy which left her unable to speak for several months prior to her passing. I wrote the following poem almost a year and a half after her death:

SOLUTIONS

Used a saline solution this morning,
Remembered your saying, "Dan, it will clear your head."
That was when you could speak--

Before the tracheotomy.
Fifteen months have passed since your demise-
Still trying to clear our heads

Searching for a solution to losing someone you love.
Are you lonesome tonight?
You sang dressed as Elvis strumming your guitar;
That, too, was before the tracheotomy.
How we hoped that doctors could reverse it.
Lying in the hospital you wrote messages on a
tiny chalkboard
We prayed as the hospital searched for a solution.
Brave you were to the end letting us know every day
How much you loved us.
If only a saline solution could cure a broken heart.

Marge as Elvis at her granddaughter Katie's wedding

Hector Gordon Pieretti, Jr.... November 2, 1940-January 23, 2016

Hector Gordon Pieretti, a man for all seasons. I knew him for over fifty years. Friend, cohort, counselor, advisor, mentor. And, from Shakespeare's Hamlet, "In action, how like an angel."

That chiseled Roman face, that clarity of thought, that precise use of language. We taught together; we were classroom cohorts, team teachers. There was a chemistry between us that elevated the content we were teaching and excited students about learning. We sparred for who would play **Macbeth** or **Hamlet** in the classroom. They were wonderful days, some of Hector Gordon's happiest, I believe. I often thought that he viewed life as a game of chess, an ongoing battle requiring a carefully thought-out game plan of strategic moves. He, of course, was the commander-in-chief responsible for the assignments, logistics, and outcomes. I am convinced that if he had been in charge during the historic Trojan War, Hector would have been the victor, not Achilles!

Yes, he was a warrior, a commander, a leader whose impact on the Greater Egg Harbor Regional High School District was enormous. As a teacher and chief administrator he truly made a difference in the lives of students, teachers and the communities serving Oakcrest and Absegami.

You may be wondering about my earlier statement…"In action how like an angel…" For me, there was an extraordinary encounter when my father died in 1995. I was at home and my wife Maria was away in New York for the day when I received word that my father had died. I remember pacing the floor and crying, and I remember a knock on the door; it was Gordon who came to comfort me. The two of us listened to the golden voice of Leontyne Price. Yes, I was touched by an angel as many of you sitting here today were touched by that same remarkable man whose special gifts, talents, love, presence and memory will serve to lift our spirits and help us face tomorrow as we remember. May he rest in peace.

Virginia Kuhn Kramer....November 14, 1941-June 2, 2016

Welcome to a very special gathering of family and friends remembering and honoring Ginny Kuhn Kramer.

Dear Ginny,

Thought a lot about you these past few days. You really caught us off-guard. I'm reminded of your first high school meeting with Maria in 1955 which bonded a lifetime friendship. I'm picturing you and the other bridesmaids in pink and green at our wedding in 1964. You were all so pretty. I'm remembering the ceremonies of life we shared together, like those memorable Christmas Day dinners at the Kramers with your famous crab dip, whisky sours, and that special floral arrangement that you created for the chandelier. The Sunday Times Crossword Puzzle and your calls to Maria to help figure out one of the answers, your sense of humor, your love for your family, your children, grandchildren. Your ending a phone conversation with "Love you." Your beautiful smile, your probing mind, our over the telephone book discussions, particularly about Hosseini's **The Kite Runner** and **A Thousand Splendid Suns.** How his words lifted our spirits in much the same way as your beautiful presence lifted ours on so many occasions.

Kahlil Gibran expresses our feelings well at this moment when he says, "Ever has it been that love knows not its own depth until the hour of separation." And, from Ernest Hemingway's **For Whom the Bell Tolls,** "How little we know of what there is to know."

And so, as the bell tolls, what we know is that we will miss you eternally. John Milton, William Blake, and Shakespeare, help us to envision the flights of angels winging Ginny beyond the Great Beyond. Godspeed.

*Ginny's two children are Christopher and Carin who is our godchild; she is a lawyer and the mother of two children, Jed and Elias.Christopher works in sales and is the father of two sons, Anthony and Chris.

Louise Levin Franklin...... April 28, 1933-July 2, 2016

Louise Levin Franklin, an American in Paris, an extraordinary citizen of the world, a world traveler, an entrepreneur, a gourmet cook, lover of Provence and all things French, a skilled eye for design and interior decorating, an aesthete, lover of the arts, cats, and pigs, a loving wife, sister, aunt, cousin, and dear dear friend. Individual and stylish, she reflected a bygone era, a lady of taste and decorum. She was true to herself and the traditions, manners and beliefs that separated her from the mainstream. Opinionated? Yes, but her opinions were hers and a perfect example for others willing to follow the strait and narrow!

Spirited and observant of life and beauty, she traveled the globe as an airline stewardess, and later in life created her very successful business TRAVEL WITH LOUISE. For any of us fortunate enough to have had her plan a trip abroad, we knew we were in the hands of a gifted purveyor who meticulously worked out the itinerary and travel connections to the last syllable. Her recommendation for the little shop in Florence that served the best gelato in the world was spot-on!

World traveler, indeed! Think of fields of lavender. Think of windmills and endless rows of tulips in Holland. Think of a feisty stewardess proving she could travel the world

with a single hatbox and ending up on the cover page of
Look magazine!

Louise really added spice and zest as she celebrated the
ceremonies of life, choreographing memorable dinner, holiday, and anniversary celebrations with family, friends, and,
especially, her Joe. If Louise was your friend, you knew it, and
she openly let you know that she loved you. Friends became
members of her family, members who shared recipes, vibrant
discussions, anecdotes, good humor, and special memories.

Louise herself is a special memory. Now away from the pain
and turmoil of earthly living, she is traveling once again, but
this time she is traveling beyond the stars and into the hands
of her Heavenly Father.

 Every little breeze will always whisper LOUISE.

May she rest in peace.

* *

*After Louise died, her husband Joe moved to Brandell
Estates, an assisted living center in Linwood, New Jersey.
We visited him often and celebrated his birthdays with the
Ravelli family from Haddonfield. Joe passed away, at nine-
ty-one, on March 26, 2020, during the Corona Virus-19
pandemic.

Mary Ellen Roken Schurtz.....March 1, 1952-July 17, 2017

Memory helps to sustain us at times like this. And who could
ever forget the beautiful memory that was, is, and will always
be Mary Ellen Schurtz. Vibrant, passionate, calming and
intuitive, " *she walked in beauty like the night of cloudless
climes and starry skies, and all that was best of dark and
bright met in her aspect* and *her eyes.*" A gentle woman with

a practical air, a love for sport, history and life, she was a loving and enviable wife to Tom and mother to their beautiful children, all their pretty chickens. Yes, she was the heart and hearth of her family in whom she instilled essential life lessons and truths to guide them. And, what a brood they have turned out to be.

Letting go was not easy as Mary Ellen courageously held on; she taught us about living and dying. Remarkably wise, she had internalized that simple truth in Antoine de Saint-Exupery's ***The Little Prince***: "*It is only with the heart that one can see rightly; what is essential is invisible to the eye.*"

As Mary Ellen continues her journey, I am reminded of a vivid moment in Alex George's novel, ***Setting Free the Kites.*** Young Nathan's father loved flying kites, but what he loved more was allowing a kite to climb higher and higher into the heavens; and, when it was no longer visible, he would cut the string, freeing it from all earthly clutter. Later in the novel, Nathan's father accidentally dies from a fall, and as a tribute to his memory, Nathan sets a kite in flight, and when that kite rose far beyond the human eye, Nathan cut the string.

In his brilliant work, ***Shadow of the Wind,*** Ruiz Zafon reminds us that "***sometimes what matters isn't what one gives but what one gives up, and as long as* we *are being remembered, we remain alive.*" I like to think of Mary Ellen that way. I know that that Christmas photograph of the Schurtz family will bring tears without its matriarch, but never fear. Her image will always be in that photograph, for as long as she is remembered, she will remain alive. Let's perform one final act to insure her longevity. Join me and all of the Schurtzes, and Rokens, and all those who have come to pay tribute to a grand lady. Grab hold of that ball of string attached to a magnificent heaven-bound kite! Let's sing and dance as the winds aloft carry that kite skyward, higher and higher and higher reaching far beyond our earthly vision. And, at the right moment one of the kite runners will reach into a pocket for an instrument to sever the string freeing Mary Ellen as she comes face to face with her Heavenly Father.

Death leaves a heartache no one can heal;
Love leaves a memory no one can steal.

(An old Irish Proverb)

Elizabeth (Betty) Dimattia.....May 5, 1924–May 25, 2018

Betty DiMattia…She was the original ever-ready battery. She simply kept going! Fred had set the stage stressing that you need to get up and once you are up, you have got to keep moving! And her daughter Linda went right along with the philosophy; she had no choice—Betty kept her moving! Dear Betty—she was one of a kind, and somehow for all her years, she was quite contemporary, very modern, up to the minute. A bit of a fashion plate, I might say! She never looked her age because she was ageless. She drove a car into her nineties. She always appeared fashionable, a lady of style and good taste.

Her family adored her and she adored them. She once told Maria and me that her son Chuck would call her every morning just checking to see if she was still alive. He didn't get the best of her, though. Chuck told us that if she didn't hear from him she would call him to see if he was alive. She was fun and had a good sense of humor. She really loved her family and would take out her cell phone and, yes, scroll through her pictures to share photos of her grandchildren and the latest great grandchild. She knew exactly how many boys and girls made up the entire DiMattia family tree.

And oh how she loved her friends, especially that weekly caravan of cars parked in front of her house from which emerged her lady friends on a mission: the weekly card games! What good times they had at Betty's playing for what we hear were high stakes! Paul Cezanne's famous painting, "The Card Players," sold for $160.000.000. I am positive that if he had had a chance to paint Betty and her special friends playing cards at her table, that painting would have doubled what the original Cezanne painting sold for. Priceless!

Betty was a wonderful cook, too, and made her own pasta which she shared with us. She was proud of her children: Chuck, who kept her landscaping beautiful, especially those Knockout Roses; and Ralph, who like his father, often did repairs around the house on his visits; and, of course, Linda—her name means "beautiful" and she is. When I think of Linda, I think of the song "Stand By Me"—

How faithfully she stood by her mom.

Once Betty said to Maria and me, "Why did Fred have to go before me?" Well, now they are together, probably having their first spat in Heaven. What a grand welcoming there must be as Betty makes her way into Heaven reunited with her Fred and other family members and friends. Sadly, she passed away just before those beautiful Crape Myrtle trees in her front yard burst into bloom. But, you know, when those Crape Myrtles get around to blooming, they will be spectac-ular, and they will perfume the air in praise and everlasting memory of a beautiful lady, Elizabeth DiMattia: wife, mother, sister, grandmother, great grandmother, aunt, great aunt, and dear, dear friend. God rest her soul.

Pasquale "Charlie" Digiovanni...December 23, 1921–January 5, 2019

Maria and I attended cousin Charlie's funeral shortly after his death on January 5, 2019. Charlie's wife predeceased him by three months. I did not speak at his funeral; his very able son, Ronald, gave the eulogy at St. Michael's Roman Catholic Church in Atlantic City, New Jersey. That church holds a lot of memories for the DiGiovanni family. Charlie's father was Loreto, a brother to my wife Maria's father, Paolo. Paolo collected funds to help build St. Michael's and to form the parish, and Paolo's wife Jennie, Maria's mother, sang in the choir, and performed in local operas there; she also donated beautiful table linen and altar cloths. Charlie and Mary DiGiovanni were married at St. Michael's and so were Maria and I.

Over the years, I gained a special affection for Charlie's mother, Carmella, and Charlie's sister Victoria Formica whose eulogy is among those in this chapter; she was godmother to my wife Maria. Charlie's cemetery service was very special as he was given a funeral with full military honors. It was a sad day, and the luncheon that followed the service brought together family and friends who shared wonderful memories.

One of the memories that I shared was that whenever Maria and I attended a family get-together, cousin Charlie would invariably come up to me and say, "Danny, when are you going to write that book?" It reminded me of the day Maria asked me what I needed to complete my dissertation, and I told her that I needed an electric typewriter. Well back then, we didn't have a word processor which is what I am using to write my "book," thanks, in part, to Pasquale Charlie DiGiovanni who was persistent in encouraging me to write. Interestingly, enough, when Charlie's wife Mary passed in

October, 2018, I had begun writing my "book" and made it a point to give a copy of the first few chapters of this memoir to Charlie in which I mention him and his influence. His son Ronnie, who gave the eulogy at Charlie's funeral, told me that he had read those chapters to Charlie. I was very happy that he got to hear them.

On the small card handed out at the church on the day of Charlie's funeral, there was a beautiful "In Loving Memory" message, along with a picture of Pasquale "Charlie" DiGiovanni…December 23, 1921-January 5, 2019. The message from his family read:

We'll always remember
that special smile, that caring heart
that warm embrace you always gave us.
You being there for mom and us through
good and bad times no matter what.
We'll always remember you, Dad, because
there'll never be anyone to replace you in
our hearts and the love we will always have for you.

Thomas H. Schurtz…..July 20, 1950-January 7, 2019

We simply were not ready for your departure. I had only begun to put away the Christmas decorations, the lighted wreaths, and the special ornaments on the tree. Maria and I had sent you a Christmas letter for 2018, remembering your annual letters and family portraits with all those beautiful faces. At the end of each Christmas season I band together the collection of cards received. Yours is among them this year with the single word JOY capturing the spirit of the season in a photograph of you and your girls, Samantha, Summer and Saylor wishing a Merry Christmas.

Happy New Year came and went, and on the seventh day of January you took your leave without warning, without a good-bye. I heard about your passing from our good friend Chuck Breitzman. How I recall and miss those A.M. chats before classes at Absegami with just the three of us, sort of like the three musketeers.

I was the luckiest musketeer of all, for I visited your class-room and watched as you mesmerized students, challenging them to look beyond the grade. You were passionate about teaching, and as I said at your retirement, you were larger than life, a formidable presence who might be described as "full of sound and fury"-but, in this case, signify-ing something.

And, of course, I cannot think of you without conjuring images from our favorite play, **Our Town** where the Stage Manager reminds the audience, "Something is eternal, and it ain't houses, and it ain't names, and it ain't earth, and it ain't even the stars…Everybody knows that something is eternal, and that something has to do with human beings."

How human you were, and from the Bard that description that fits you like a glove: "What a piece of work is a man. How noble in reason! How infinite in faculty! In form, in moving, how express and admirable! In action how like an angel. In apprehension how like a God."

And at your first retirement, here is how I described you:

Tom Schurtz, teacher, actor, director, devotee of
Shakespeare, captivated by the words, ideas, images
and themes, convoluted plots and incestuous relation-
ships. Kings and Queens and fops, and all of life's
menagerie parading for Tom the Magnificent dressed
in borrowed robes determined to shake his gory locks

at unsuspecting students doomed to internalize
Shakespeare's eternal mutterings forever!

And so, Tom Schurtz, the rest is silence as you embark on your final retirement, perhaps arriving at the Pearly Gates in that never-to-be-forgotten white suit making an indelible impression as Saint Peter takes your hand.

With Deep Affection,

DOC

*All four children of Tom and Mary Ellen Schurtz worked as aides in my English Office at Absegami High School. They are Thomas Jr., Kathleen, Robert, and Stephen. As I write this memoir, Kathleen is presently the Supervisor of English at Absegami, Tom, Jr. is an English teacher, and Robert is a vice-principal. Stephen works in sales and was expecting his first child in July, 2019. The Schurtzes are a remarkable family and over the years became an extended family of ours.

Joseph Peter Tozzi....December 21, 1940--October 22, 2019

Giuseppe Tozzi

A simple, unpretentious man, Joe Tozzi was not interested in throngs of people at his funeral, just those closest to him, those that he considered la famiglia, family. Naturally humorous, he would remind us, "You've got to have a sense of humor." Honored as a citizen of the year, he was actually a man for all ages. Practical and smart, he prided himself as a numbers man, and my how he was able to calculate! Like a character from the Silver Screen which he adored, his life itself was a story worthy of being filmed or written about. His is a great American tale about a young boy who lived with his grandmother in Philadelphia, a blind grandmother whom he gave insulin shots. Transported to Atlantic City, that young boy had a dream and worked numerous jobs night and day determined never to be poor, becoming a man with a vision that he transformed into an empire.

Charitable to a fault, his generosity extended to those in need, numerous organizations and individuals, including American Indians and South American children living in poverty whom he sponsored and watched grow up through the Children's International Program.

He loved the music of the 50's and literally lit up when he heard a recording of "Stagger Lee." His favorite holiday was Christmas for which he prepared thousands of Pizzelles that he delivered annually, at Christmas, driving his sleigh, his Chevy Tahoe. He also drove that sleigh to gather a truckload of holly for us; the last delivery was two days before he had a stroke on December 20th, 2018, one day before his birthday. He loved children. He loved Pete, his German Shepherd; he loved the ducks out at Birch Grove Park; he loved the rabbits in his backyard; he loved his children, his family, and special friends.

One day when he, Maria and I were traveling somewhere in his truck, he was telling us a story. At one point, he couldn't think of a word he needed, and as he struggled to find it, he finally blurted out, "Hocus Pocus!" I was in the back seat and literally collapsed laughing. I still laugh when I think of that moment. There was another hilarious moment I will never forget. One afternoon I was working in the downstairs of his building; he was upstairs, at the time, watching the film **South Pacific.** Suddenly he threw open the door singing, "Some Enchanted Evening," a song from the film. I roared with laughter and shortly thereafter called Maria to tell her that Rossano Brazzi had just paid me a visit! The kicker to that wonderful story is that I recently found out that Rossano Brazzi's voice in the film was dubbed, and the singer was a Metropolitan star named Giorgio Tozzi, perhaps a long-lost cousin of Joe's.

What a sense of humor! I'd like to be able to wish him back again using "hocus pocus" or some other incantation, but I know that is not possible. His sons have a lot to live up to. Giuseppe, how lucky all of us here are to have known you as a friend, as a mentor, as a relative, as an advisor, as a business-man, as a giving human being always willing to put others before yourself. We will miss your humor, your tenacity, your good taste, your eye for beauty, your sense of correctness, your rules for life, and the realization that there will never ever be another Joe Tozzi. God rest your soul.

* *

It is with deep gratitude that I remember all of the remark-able individuals who comprise this Gallery of Eulogies. Equally memorable are those no longer living and previously highlighted or eulogized within the body of this memoir:

Hilda S. Frame, teacher and inspiration, eulogized in Chapter 4.

Uncle Leo Landy, adopted uncle, husband of Hazel, inspira-tion for *A Swinger of Cattails*, eulogized in Chapter 8.

Victor R. Walters, my brother who died tragically from an accident, prompting the original sonnet in his memory, Chapter 16.

Louisa Craig and Tom Craig (Grandpa Tucker), adopted grandparents, special references to them in Chapter 16 and Chapter 23.

Phyllis Walters Azzara, my brother's wife who raised their children after his death, remaining a close family member, eulogized in Chapter 16.

Jennie DiGiovanni, Maria's mother, my mother-in-law, whom I celebrated in a summer's ending piece entitled *As Summer Slips Away*, Chapter 19.

Princess Diana, mother of William and Andrew, honored in an original poem, *A Spenserian Stanza*, Chapter 20.

Paul Giovanni, brother-in-law, eulogized in *A Man for All Seasons*, Chapter 21.

Jim O'Brien, weatherman celebrated in Chapter 22, *Goldenrod*.

I can't help but wonder how different my journey might have been had it not been for the influence and love of all of these amazing people. I often wish that I could make contact with one or more of them and must admit that I have, on occasion, looked for a sign from one of them. An interesting occurrence at Mother Brown's viewing in June, 1993, which was held at the Old Union Hotel where I grew up in Nesco, New Jersey, was relayed to me by Linda Spendiff, a former student and long-standing friend. Sometime after the funeral, Linda asked me who the little girls were whom she observed near my mother's casket. I was perplexed and probed her further and learned about her paranormal ability. I did not see the little girls but recalled an old photograph of young children found in the attic of the Old Union Hotel. Perhaps there was some connection. Maria has said on more than one occasion that if there is any way that someone who has died can make contact with the living, her mother Jennie would be the one to do it.

An ADC sign (an After Death Communication) is not uncommon, and, interestingly enough, the "butterfly" is the most frequently mentioned ADC sign. In many spiritual circles, that beautiful creature represents the spirit or soul; it is a spiritual symbol for life after death. And so, another of my "end of summer" pieces serves as a perfect conclusion to this chapter. The piece was written in November, 1981, and is entitled **Monarch Migration**.

MONARCH MIGRATION

A single, beautiful Monarch butterfly circled my Montpelier Avenue backyard, ending summer on a Sunday morning in early November. I had just finished raking and bagging thousands of dried maple leaves that insisted on blowing in all directions of a weather vane, and upon walking to my backyard--where I surveyed my garden's summer's end—the butterfly suddenly appeared.

I stood in awe, never expecting to see such a creature so late in autumn, remembering one day five years ago in early October when a migration of Monarchs passed over city and countryside as it colorfully streamed its way south away from fall and winter. This November butterfly, however, darted from one corner of my yard to another, flew over the fence into my neighbor's yard, then sailed back to me again, overhead, over the fence, over summer. Gone.

Watching it fly away, I couldn't help but wonder if this Monarch had been part of the yearly migration, having lost its way, or, perhaps, this single orange and black milkweed beauty was the lead flyer in a late wave of migrants called upon by some spiritual force to fill the void of a dying earth whose brittled past I had stuffed into hefty trash bags. Or, perhaps, this butterfly had been a late bloomer, a curious soul, a loner who hears a different drummer and dares to strike out on his own, purposely losing the crowd: a non-conformist for whom conformity is an aversion and for whom the desire to be an individual transcends all other earthly passions. Then again, perhaps the lonely flutterer considered Montpelier Avenue a perfect Sunday meeting place where one could commune with God, and on this particular Sunday in November flew in to take one last fleeting look at summer's passing in my backyard.

Here is what we saw: Unripened tomatoes on limp, dying vines. Orange-faced marigolds mourning summer's end. A stately French lilac browned by heat but tipped with terminal buds, asleep until spring. White and red geraniums holding on until a killing frost. Rose bushes long past the last rose of summer. Sweet basil matured to columns of dried seeds. The apple tree defoliated by a natural sequence of seasonal events. And, flowering Impatiens of white and pink, one of the last hardy summer survivors awaiting that one chilling night when it will patiently surrender.

Yes, a single solitary Monarch butterfly saw all that with me on a sun-warmed November autumn morning, and then flew away. With it went summer which, for one beautiful moment, had been metamorphosed into a circling Monarch Butterfly in flight, marking the end of a season.

25

HANDS OF GOLD

Over the course of our marriage, Maria and I have delighted in meeting and knowing a variety of people and families. One of the most remarkable families is the Higbee family with whom Maria first became acquainted at Oakcrest High school in 1963. That was the year she began teaching and observed the handwriting of one of her freshmen students, Herbert Lawrence Higbee. Her interest in his handwriting stemmed from what she observed to be similar to that of her father, Paolo DiGiovanni, whose distinct script mirrored that of someone born in Europe. Sure enough, Maria learned that Herbert and his family had recently arrived back in America after having lived in France for several years where he had learned to speak the language as well as adopt a particular method of hand-writing.

Over the four years of high school, we became better acquainted with Herbert. Before I met him, I had directed his sister Susan in a Thornton Wilder play entitled *The Happy Journey from Trenton to Camden*. Herbert also expressed an interest in drama and became quite active in the Oakcrest Drama Club which Maria and I directed. It turned out that he could sing and dance which led to a lead role in an original musical version of the English farce, *Charley's Aunt*, written by Brandon Thomas. To our surprise, his talents also included construction skills which he used to help build sets for our drama productions, including *Charley's Aunt* and *Carnival*.

Our connection with Herbert continued to grow, and at some point we found out that he was also known as Larry. We kept in touch over the years, and he became the go-to person whom Maria identified years after his graduation from American University as a potential designer for laying out the specifications for what was to become the annual Margate Fall Funfest begun in 1998. His map of the targeted site for the city blocks proposed for the event was drawn to scale, identifying component elements, including spaces for participating food and merchandise vendors. Maria's plan for decorating the proposed site included haystacks and cornstalks which Larry also included in his overall drawing of the site. Because of Larry's meticulous attention to detail, the city commissioners applauded and accepted the plan which opened the door to the Margate Fall Funfest which debuts annually in late September.

We have maintained a close relationship with Larry who worked as the technical director for entertainment at the Tropicana Hotel and Casino in Atlantic City, and as a technical director for trade shows and creative advisor for the Atlantic City Coin and Slot Service Company. His interest in theatre has continued as he is often recruited to build sets for local theatre productions.

In the fall of 2018, Maria and I traveled to Vermont with Larry to visit a former student and classmate, Diane Kemble Co-Francesco, who was active in the Oakcrest Drama Club as a wardrobe mistress. During our visit, we reminisced about some of the drama productions, recalling Larry's performances as Dr. Glass in the production of *Carnival,* and Charles Wykeham in *Charley's Aunt*. Of particular interest in the programs for those drama productions were printed ads which helped pay for the cost of printed programs. One of those ads read:

ALICE HIGBEE VOICE STUDIO
Specialized Instruction for
SINGERS-----------------SPEAKERS
SPEECH THERAPY
By Appointment Only

Alice was Larry's mother, and if Larry had hands of gold, so did his father and his mother who also had a golden voice. At some point back in the 1960's or 1970's, Maria and I visited with Larry's parents at a house that was being built for the family. There was much to be done, and I learned that the house was being constructed as a tribute to Alice Higbee from her husband, L. Herbert Higbee. I was very moved by the underlying love story for the construction of the house and found out that Mr. Higbee traveled from New Jersey to Canada to retrieve rocks for the house he was building for Alice. Sadly, she died on June 25, 1975 before the house was completed. I sought to capture the amazing story of Mr. Higbee in October, 1982, in an end-of summer piece entitled ***Journeying North and South.***

JOURNEYING NORTH AND SOUTH

Two significant events combined a shape and a journey that marked the end of summer on October sixth, 1982. The first was the dependable "V" of an early morning flock of geese winging south. The second event, a journey begun in the early hours before the geese had arrived over West Atlantic City, was a sojourn north by a man in the autumn of his life, traveling from New Jersey to Canada in search of a rock quarry. It was as if one event had triggered the other, unbeknownst to man or bird in a universe of coincidence. That both should have just happened to occur on the same day punctuated the opportunity to sketch in word or color, a perfect blend to a summer's end.

Think of the power of the images, for a moment. First, birds intuitively striking out to escape the rush of autumn and prolonged cold, sky barometers of the air signaling the ending of a season. Couple that image with an aging man trucking north to retrieve specially selected Canadian rocks to be used to continue building a mansion he had begun years ago as a tribute to his beloved wife who, in the midst of his labor, contracted a disease that led to her death, an early frost that deadened the spirit and hope of her beloved husband.

For years the house has sat, an incomplete monument weathered by springs and summers and falls and winters, each season crueler than the ones past. But then, on this October sixth, as another summer ended, Mr. Higbee rallied as if to reverse the change of seasons, or to prolong summer just long enough to begin anew the task he had begun in transporting those special rocks for his and her house so many summers ago.

As he traveled north, those southward bound geese overhead must have wondered why one would be heading that way, rather than in their direction. He himself must have pondered their magnificence and the array of New England reds and yellows and burnt oranges in his travelogue of autumnal color. Perhaps both figures in these two significant events, man and bird, contributed to the will-power of the other; for the awesome spirit of both is a mark of determination and undying strength.

For sure, Canadian geese will fly north and south again at the cue of changing seasons. And, somehow, the beauty and memory of Mrs. Higbee will never die. Memories linger; monuments are constructed to last. Mr. Higbee will have seen to that. Rocks loaded from the quarry precipitate the return journey south to the little town of Sculville in Southern New Jersey where there is work to be done before winter's cold sets in and before Canadian geese once again fly north. In their return flight, they are bound to espy an aging man, hard at work, in the autumn of his life, lifting and setting rocks from their homeland to build his own as he approaches another spring and summer and awaits a call from the North.

*Mr. Higbee died on July 7, 1986. The house he was building as a tribute to his wife Alice was still under construction at the time of his death.

* *

Mr. Higbee's journey was a different one from mine although there are parallels. Like him, I spent a lifetime at work; we were both builders. He was building a house, and I helped to build Oakcrest and Absegami High Schools. He had dreams of a better life when he gathered his family and moved to France where he found employment. I had dreams of a better life, lifting myself up to become something; that something turned out to be a teacher. My search for a definition of what I had become will be the subject of another chapter influenced, in part, by Dr. Adam Pfeffer to whom I wrote an important letter on December 1, 2004, seven months before my retirement.

(26)

A LETTER TO THE BOARD OF EDUCATION

December 1, 2004

Board of Education
Greater Egg Harbor Regional High School Distric
1820 Dr. Dennis Foreman Drive
Mays Landing, New Jersey 08330

Dear Dr. Pfeffer and Members of the Board,

As I draft this letter of retirement I am thinking about Alpha, the Class of 1964, Oakcrest's first four-year graduating class which will hold its fortieth reunion on November 13. I began my years of service to the district in September, 1962, and I remember those Alpha Falcons and the joy of teaching and soaring with them; I was a fledgling beginning a career. It was also at Oakcrest where I met my dear Maria, and we were married on June 20, 1964—another recent forty-year celebration. How we loved our years in the district, celebrating life, youth, and the joy of teaching.

My personal desire to teach was seeded years ago in the Hilda S. Frame School in Mullica Township, a two-room school where an extraordinary teacher nurtured this young ward of the state and made a difference that no one can ever fully calculate. I like to think that I, too, have had some measurable impact on the lives of teachers and the thousands of students whom I have taught and loved, the thousands whose special gifts were an invitation to be the best teacher possible as I challenged intellect, molded character and dreams, and realized that my mission as an educator would be a life-time occupation.

Now a hybrid—a Brave Falcon—having lived through countless migrations of birds traveling north and south, having observed over 700 moons, having taught more than 7,000 days, having given 40 years of educational service, and looking forward to a life-time of great expectations, I announce my plan to take my leave, to retire, effective July 1, 2005.

My sincerest thanks to an august Board and the colleagues, administrators, and life-long friends whom I will always remember with deep affection.

Sincerely,

Dr. Daniel N. Walters

cc: Mr. Raymond Dolton, Principal
Mr. Thomas Grossi, Secretary/Business Administrator

RISING WITH MAYA ANGELOU, GUEST SPEAKER, AND A BROKEN SHOULDER

Having submitted my letter of retirement, I felt a bit nostalgic thinking about where I had begun my journey and how many miles I had traveled since. I still had loads to lift before my final days as a supervisor of five departments at Absegami High School: English, Reading, Drama, Media and Dance. Over the years from 1962 through 2005, I had supervised more than fifty teachers, including some from the Foreign Language Department. I was very proud of my staff and the effort displayed in building curricula, integrating creativity and the arts into daily teaching, responding to state educational mandates, and constructing assessment materials which proved challenging and engaging, fostering critical thinking, creativity, and concrete methods for measuring student performance. As lofty as those aims were, I came to realize that the staff members in my departments had become like family. And, I recalled the phrase in loco parentis from one of my educational courses; teaching was an all-consuming profession in which "teacher" often became a parental figure. At this turning point in my life, I thought about all the years I had been a teacher and how often students had reached out to me for guidance. I remembered instances when I was able to draw upon my own life experience to help students living in foster or broken homes.

Students were the heart of the school, and I was honored to be the speaker for the Anthony J. Panarelle Chapter of the National Honor Society induction ceremony held on April 19, 2005 in the Absegami High School auditorium where I gave the following presentation:

NATIONAL HONOR SOCIETY INDUCTION CEREMONY

April 19, 2005

In 1957 I was inducted into the Hammonton High School Chapter of the National Honor Society. I remember tears, and I remember being proud. I had overcome another hurdle in my own life. I can say that now looking back because there were numerous hurdles that had brought me to that moment. I was raised as a ward of the state, my mother having deserted her three children many years before. The toughest part about growing up as a ward of the state was not knowing how long it would be before my brother, sister or I would be leaving one set of foster parents and moving on to another. We became separated at times. As a result of that bumpy childhood, I remember no schooling before second grade which I believe was at the Port Republic School. I moved three more times after Port Republic and finally ended up in Nesco, a little town out near Hammonton. To make a long story short, a teacher at the Nesco Grammar School took me under wing, and I began to rise, in much the same way as Maya Angelou talks about "rising" in her extraordinary poem, "Still I Rise," in which she lyrically expresses bitterness and pain transformed by inner strength, depth of character, and the conquering of hurdles.

What a fitting message for you inductees from a great American poet "welling and swelling and bearing the tide," rising up against any obstacle, challenging a sometimes cruel and myopic world with prejudice aimed to knock her down. For me, it was "the state kid"; for Maya, it was a past rooted in pain, a victim of unkind words and hatefulness, aiming to see her broken.

What a message here on the 19th of April 2005 for you inductees having risen to the occasion through your scholarship, your service, your leadership, and your character, each one of those qualities singularly significant but altogether helping you to rise to a new height, helping you to set the stage for personal hurdles to be overcome as you continue to grow, to give, to care about others, to actively participate as a citizen, to dream, to hope, to rise.

If you read Maya Angelou's *I Know Why the Caged Bird Sings*, you will appreciate even more the human struggle to survive. That struggle for survival and longing to be free parallels, perhaps, the struggle of that remarkable flower or weed finding a way to rise up and break through a crevice in the concrete of a playground in the middle of a city. What a hurdle! How did that flower or weed manage to survive? How did Maya Angelou manage to survive? How will you manage to survive?

The answer to those questions lies in the challenges that you will face and how you will handle them tomorrow. Without being too preachy I might suggest that you take a good look in the mirror of life, and as you reflect on your accomplishments, be proud—yes—but give some thought to the next steps of your journey and how your National Honor Society membership will enable you to rise to even greater heights as you become leaders in your community helping to create a fair playing field for all people, as you give service through organizations aimed to provide for the good and welfare of others, as you recognize scholarship as a life-long activity making you a life-long learner more interested in learning than memorizing, and as you display character by being true to yourself, committed to worthy values, and willing to stand up for what you believe.

And so, as the caged bird sings, allow its melody and the lighted candles of this evening's induction to light your way in the future as you use the gifts of your ancestors and the empowering strength of Scholarship, Leadership, Service and Character to overcome life's hurdles, to magnify your purpose, to realize your hopes and dreams, and to face the world proudly and say, "I rise."

The day that I gave the presentation for the National Honor Society induction was nine days after I had an accidental fall in New York City at the Javits Center where Maria and I were attending a spring linen show. My fall occurred as the result of someone failing to tack down a piece of metal stripping on a platform. Unfortunately, we had taken a bus to New York and after my fall I was taken to Saint Vincent's Hospital where I was x-rayed and given a pain-killer before I was released. The hospital confirmed that I had a broken shoulder, and Maria and I made our way out to the streets of New York to hail a taxi to take us to the Port Authority Bus Terminal where we boarded a bus for a most uncomfortable ride to Atlantic City.

I fell on April 10, 2005, roughly two and one-half months before my July 1st. retirement date. I knew what lay ahead for the next two months; I had to close out an academic school year and complete preparations for whoever would replace me. Closing down the year included the completion of annual evaluations for twenty-seven teachers. I was responsible for inventorying thousands of textbooks and orchestrating their return to a departmental bookroom. I had to inventory and assist in the retrieval of audio-visual equipment, some of which were housed in the Media Center. I was responsible for generating a list of courses for the five content areas that I supervised, along with the creation of a tentative fall schedule for each of the staff members. I worked closely with Bob Quinn, Guidance Supervisor, in building tentative teacher schedules as part of a master schedule for the following academic year. All of those tasks were essential, and I was determined not to allow a broken humerous to keep me from fulfilling my responsibilities—as funny as that might sound! Because of the nature of the break in my shoulder, no cast was involved. Fortunately, it was my left shoulder, and I am right-handed. However, I could not begin therapy until late June. That meant a lot of icing, the use of a sling, and hitching rides to school since I could not drive a car. It also meant requiring assistance in getting dressed—special thanks to my dear wife for her help.

To my own amazement, I managed to complete all of the tasks noted above although my year ended in late June after all of the other supervisors had left for the summer. My broken shoulder was a painful ordeal which required me to sit up in a chair (Maria's father's chair) where I slept for a three month period.

This is a perfect moment to applaud and to thank the following members of my departments whose assistance during this difficult period enabled me to complete the monumental tasks related to closing down a school year and a forty year career:

Scott Alten	Denise Khoury
Dee Bailey	Shannon McKittrick
Chuck Breitzman	Becky McMurray
Judy Callahan	Scott Parker
Tina Canesi	Michael Piotrowski
Larry Caplan	Denise Price
Dorsey Finn	Lori Ranck
Mandy Franklin	Carolyn Rosenberger
Chip Garrison	Tom Schurtz
Kristine Greenfield	Sandy Segal
Linda Gronlund	Lynne Silvestro
Jeremy Harp	Michelle TenBrook
Jaime Howey	Lisa Zeuner
Ed Johnson	

28

DEFINING TEACHERS

Dr. Adam Pfeffer, the superintendent for the Greater Egg Harbor Regional High School District, gave me an assignment some time in the 1990's. The task was to define TEACHER, and I consciously found myself thinking about the defining attributes, keeping a file of notes, and, on several occasions, writing about teachers whose talents held the potential for helping me fulfill Dr. Pfeffer's assignment. One such teacher, an English teacher in my department, retired before I did, and in 1999 had been selected as Absegami's "Teacher of the Year." She was a remarkable educator, and upon her "teacher of the year" selection, I spoke about her accomplishments.

Margaret Guenther

> This is a eulogy for the living, one Margaret Guenther, in particular. I've checked the dictionary, and I made a quick check before leaving school this afternoon at which time Mrs. Guenther appeared to be well and alive, and so I've decided to eulogize her!
>
> Now I didn't have to look into her room to discern her state of mortality. Let me explain. It was right after lunch that I heard that familiar screeching but enviable vocal instrument of hers—her voice—thundering "Sinners in the Hands of An Angry God" echoing into the hallways and through an eighteen inch thick wall, interrupting my usual nod-off which,

fortunately, saved me from the wrath of Dr. Mackie, our principal, who happened to be passing by my office at the time.

That makes her a heroine of sorts, doesn't it? That's why we're here, isn't it? Yes, her voice is unmistakable and truly capable of awakening the dead: Shakespeare, Jonathan Edwards, Nathaniel Hawthorne, Emily Dickinson, Mark Twain—she has brought them all to life in that classroom of hers. And, her voice is equally capable of awakening the living, all of us here, today, who in some way have been moved to a realization about her as an exceptional teacher and human being, someone who inspires students and colleagues, alike, through her presence, her sense of right and wrong, her knowledge and wisdom, her good common sense, her tenacity, her sense of order, her demanding nature, her bill of rights, her sense of humor, and her compelling leadership.

For all of those qualities, in part, she joins the parade of teachers extraordinaire who validate a profession that many of us here, today, perceive as a calling to minister to the hearts, hurts, and minds of children maturing into young adults.

I have said to Mrs. Guenther, on more than one occasion, that I would have loved to have been one of her students, and in a way I have been. Dr. Pfeffer, she has enhanced my search for that elusive definition of the word, TEACHER.

Teacher: Someone whose very presence evokes an interest and invitation to learning.

Teacher: Someone who leads you to think about things that you never even thought of, or that you never knew you could think about.

Teacher: Someone who lifts the human spirit, and by so doing rises to higher ground.

Teacher: Someone who leaves us with indelible impressions—like red wheelbarrows and elixirs of life.

Teacher: Someone who teaches us the difference between right and wrong without preaching it.

Teacher: Someone who magically suspends time and reality for purposes that extend human consciousness.

Teacher: Someone who is larger than life and helps others transcend the humdrum of everyday life.

Teacher: Someone who challenges you to stand on your own two feet and formulate an original thought.

Teacher: Someone who allows you to be yourself and to grow a foot or more through deliberate pruning and cultivation.

AND FINALLY,

Teacher: Someone who skillfully weaves stories that lead to an awareness of enduring values and understandings of life.

Mrs. Guenther, you are that story-teller, that creator of indelible impressions, that challenge to mind and spirit, that worker of the soil who deliberately prunes and cultivates and has helped to nurture generations of wheelbarrow pushers whom you have led to think about things that they would never have thought about. Congratulations, we salute you as Absegami's Teacher of the Year!

＊ ＊

Mrs. Guenther is still living as I write this memoir. Sadly, another defining teacher, Thomas Henry Schurtz, passed away on January 7, 2019; a eulogy that I composed for him appears in Chapter 24. Tom had declared that when I retired, he would also retire, and he did. He, too, had been honored as a Teacher of the Year. Truly one of a kind, he could be considered a "teacher's teacher." I had the privilege of speaking at his retirement dinner in 2005.

On Thomas Schurtz Retiring

TOM THUMB   THOMAS WOLFE   THOMAS AQUINAS

TOM BUCHANAN   TOMMY LASOURDA   TOM SAWYER

TOM CRAIG   TOM PIOTROWSKI   SIR THOMAS MALORY

TOM SCHURTZ

Linked by a common name, a roster of uncommon characters playing out their parts dictated by time and fate, invention, craft, imagination, inspiration, and profession. Some are characters of fiction, one or more a writer of fiction. A holy man, a Nesco farmer, a sports figure, a giant of a man, and one—without a doubt—a quintessential veteran teacher whose amazing talents and contributions as teacher, mentor, coach, colleague, family man, and friend are what we are celebrating today. Tom Schurtz, who is larger than life, is a formidable presence and might be described as "full of sound and fury"—but, in this case, signifying something.

That "something" is, in part, the eternal search by great writers and thinkers like Edith Hamilton in the **Ever-Present Past** where antiquity houses the essential truths about who and what we are. That message is echoed again in Act 3 of one of Tom's all-time favorite plays, Our Town, where the Stage Manager reminds us that "Something is eternal, and it ain't houses, and it ain't names, and it ain't earth, and it ain't even the stars… Everybody knows in their bones that something is eternal, and that that something has to do with human beings…There's something way down deep that's eternal about every human being."

There is something eternal about a teacher who stirs imaginations and spirits about the Legend of King Arthur, the Code of Chivalry, and the creation of original heraldry. Sir Thomas Schurtz launched the search for the Holy Grail while awakening imaginations and the spirit of the eternal quest, galloping forward in search of it each September for the past thirty-three years.

Turning another page, I see on the horizon a figure in white galloping full speed ahead. Can it be? Is it? Yes, it is! Tom Quixote, the quixotic and romantic adventurer dreaming the impossible dream, teaching *Macbeth* to an auditorium full of Newark kids at Central High, circling the prickly pear with T.S. Eliot, reliving Martin Luther King's "I've Got A Dream" speech with an eager bunch of freshmen whom Mr. Schurtz transports back in time to a time when life was both more simple and more complex as he searches for the key using eternal and practical truths to teach those at risk a sense of self-respect and values to be internalized for safe keeping for the future when he's not around.

Tom's love for literature and ideas and his ability to captivate, to dazzle, to keep that audience coming back has an almost Barnum and Bailey appeal. As the Ringmaster, he holds court drawing from the power of another Thomas, Thomas Carlyle, the writer-philosopher who reminds us that "Literature is the thought of thinking souls." For Tom Schurtz, thinking about literature really means immersing oneself in it, and if the opportunity arises, acting out the role of Willy Loman from Arthur Miller's *Death of A Salesman* or William Shakespeare's *Macbeth.*

Tom Schurtz: Teacher, actor, director, devotee of Shakespeare, captivated by the words, ideas, images and themes, convoluted plots and incestuous relationships, kings and queens and fops and all of life's menagerie parading for Tom the Magnificent dressed in borrowed robes determined to shake his gory locks at unsuspecting students doomed to internalize Shakespeare's eternal mutterings forever!

Oh may the Muses make merry on this special occasion. Tom Schurtz as Falstaff sweats to death and lards the earth as he walks along, and as I sing my final praise knowing that in his retirement he, like those heroic larger than life figures, will go out having the last word, fighting and grimacing, and barking and belching and farting! But, before he goes, I have one final word from the Bard:

Who is it that says most?

Which can say more than this rich praise—

That you alone are you

That you alone are you

That you alone are you, Tom Schurtz, and we love you!

29

A SURPRISE RETIREMENT DINNER

Where does the time go was uppermost in my mind when 2005 arrived, the year of my retirement. As mentioned earlier, I would end my career with a broken shoulder. As always, I was determined that any ailment, kidney stones, a tonsillectomy at age twenty-four, torn cartilage, or any other temporary malady would never keep me from moving forward. There was work to be done, and just like that moment years ago when I peered into a mirror and asked, "Who's going to get you through this?," the answer was obvious.

I was grateful for my wife Maria's assistance, along with that of colleagues and others who helped me during my recovery with the daily and practical tasks required for meeting my responsibilities. As I went about my work in late spring, little did I realize what Maria and Linda Gronlund, Lori Ranck, Tom Schurtz, and other teachers from my department were up to as they secretively made arrangements for a retirement dinner which occurred on May 6, 2005.

On the day of that surprise dinner, I went about my normal schedule of work at school-- clueless. I believed that I was going to a CARING fundraiser that our good friend Joe Tozzi had invited us to attend. Initially, I had told Maria that I really didn't feel like going to the affair. When she told Linda Gronlund that I was hedging about going, Maria told Linda that she would get me there even if she had to roll me in on a gurney! The enticement that Joe Tozzi and Maria used was crab cakes, delicious crab cakes which the Great Bay Country Club was known for. As it turned out, it was a stormy evening—actually, there was a raging nor'easter—just my kind of weather. Maria drove because of my shoulder, and, fortunately, we were able to valet park which I later learned Maria had arranged for.

I recall climbing a set of stairs at the country club with Maria holding my arm. Upon reaching the top of the stairs, there was a thunderous outburst, "Surprise!" I was truly surprised and shaken; Maria has reminded me since of how I shook. What a genuine surprise and marvelous evening of delicious food with over a hundred well-wishers. Much of the evening is a blur, but I danced with my arm in a sling and listened to comments from Tom Schurtz and Chuck Breitzman who spoke glowingly about my accomplishments, followed by several other speakers: my niece, Dorothy Baldwin, whom you'll recall from Chapter 6 of this memoir, the little girl in my "All Saints Be Praised" essay, and my cousin Marianna Martino who traditionally leaves a box of spiced wafers and a copy of *The Old Farmer's Almanac* in my mailbox. It was a 2010 copy of that almanac from Marianna that led to my national recognition when I wrote about *The Kindest Thing Anyone Ever Did For Me,* found in Chapter 2 of this memoir.

Chip Garrison, Absegami's Drama Director, spoke eloquently in a prepared delivery:

> Good evening. I just wanted to offer a remembrance of our guest of honor and his importance to the drama program. As a matter of fact, when you think about it, it really boils down to THREE WORDS. And what are the Three Words you ask? Well, let me set the stage, so to speak. It is an opening night of any of the sixty some odd productions we have now performed on the stage(s) of Absegami High School. And as anyone in show business will tell you, there is something about an opening night—the energy, the tension, the anxiety…that makes all opening nights special and unique. Backstage, my normally calm and reserved drama students (yeah, right!) are busy getting into make-up, altering costumes, learning lines…Suddenly…the THREE WORDS come from the front door, maybe from a meddling drama

parent, perhaps from an undressed usher. Like a California forest fire during a month-long drought, it spreads to the stage crew as they try to remember the difference between a flathead screwdriver and a Phillips head screwdriver. And, finally, it reaches the actors, who are in the throes of grappling with the fact that the world does not, indeed, revolve around them. The three words, ladies and gentlemen, begin in a whisper, and soon grow to an excited roar…DOC IS HERE…DOC IS HERE….DOC IS HERE!!!

The cast and crew are so excited because they know that there will be atleast ONE person in the audience who will laugh just a little louder and longer at EVERY JOKE IN THE PLAY! EVEN THE ONES THE ACTORS NEVER UNDERSTOOD THEMSELVES! They will anxiously await the dramatic moment in the play when the audience is absolutely silent except for one loud "Oahahah!" And they wait for someone to know when to clap at the end of scenes throughout the play, almost reminding the audience that they are watching a live play and not watching television at home.

The THREE WORDS. DOC IS HERE! Before every show I give a half hour pep talk to the cast, but in just those THREE WORDS I can count on the fact that the cast may finally be able to focus on what it is we're trying to do on that stage. DOC IS HERE! Thank you, Dr. Walters, for always being there on Opening Night. Thank you for laughing a little louder, clapping a little longer, and for reminding audiences that the theatre is a temple to be loved, honored and cherished. On behalf of the EMANON PLAYERS of Absegami High School, I would like to present you with the following gift: Four complimentary passes to any and all future Opening Nights of any and all future Emanon Players Productions. These four passes entitle you to what will now be known as DOC'S SEATS in ROW U, SEATS 10, 11, 12 and

13. And with the completion of the engraving, each seat will have a name plate with, you guessed it, THREE WORDS… DOC IS HERE!

⁎ ⁎

Following Chip's "Doc Is Here" presentation, Ray Dolton, Absegami's principal, paid me a wonderful compliment by saying that he didn't know how he could get along without me. I was then called up to speak, and after thanking everyone I remember quoting the opening lines of the Creed of the Freeman: "I do not wish to be a common man, it is my right to be uncommon if I can…" I then shared some of my past which is at the core of this memoir. Two teachers from the English Department then presented me with a special gift; it was an original pointillism drawing of me dressed in a red and white Santa cap with DOC inscribed on the white fur of the cap. It was a particularly special gift in that the artist was Melanie Schroer, the daughter of a former student, Fred Schroer, who was part of that amazing group of students who constructed the Grover's Corners Cemetery while we were studying Thornton Wilder's play, **Our Town**.

I mingled with friends and family, including Maria's dear cousin, Sister Theresa Kelly, M.F.A, who drove all the way from Haledon, New Jersey in spite of the weather. Her presence was a gift in itself. Another special gift was a recipe for making bread from my former principal, Anthony Panarelle, whose family owned Panarelle's Bakery located in Atlantic City next to St. Michael's Grammar School where Maria and her cousin Theresa recalled that tantalizing aroma of baking bread wafting through the air and open windows of their classrooms.

Besides those delicious crab cakes and dinner, Maria had selected perhaps the most memorable cake of my life: a huge coconut cake with a lemon filling that was truly a gift from the gods. It was baked by someone known as the Cake Lady from Marmora; that lady is definitely a national treasure! All Saints Be Praised!

I received many cards and hand-written wishes for the future. One of the sweetest was a letter from Maria's Aunt Anna Acciavatti:

To My Dear Nephew Doctor Dan Walters,

I am sorry that I cannot attend your retirement dinner given by your faculty members, dearest wife Maria, and friends. The reason is I am 91 years young and not allowed to go out at night. I would like to share a couple of thoughts about this special occasion.

It seems like it was only yesterday you were in college, then on to your master's and doctorate degree, ready to go out into the working world. You are an exceptional person, you work very hard and you knew in your heart that you wanted to become a good teacher. To be there for your students, and try to make them understand that without an education, they would never make it in today's world. You did achieve your goal.

Don't be upset about the word "retiring" because you will be working harder, trying to fit in all the things that you wanted to do for yourself when this day would arrive. You won't have to worry and you won't be alone. You will have Maria beside you, and what you won't remember to do, she will.

I wish you a healthy and happy retirement in the years to come. I love you both very much. May God Bless You and keep you in his care always.

Love you,
Aunt Anna

Shortly after that memorable retirement dinner and Aunt Anne's letter, I received another very special letter from Dr. Joe DiIenno, a long-time friend and husband of Camille Giuffre, a college friend of Maria's.

> Dan, it was a great pleasure to be present for the celebration of your teaching. I can envision you teaching and wonderfully edifying your students. Awakening young minds is a privilege. From those I spoke with, and from my own

experience, something deeper occurs when you're engaged with others. Your dignity and uniqueness get communicated to them beyond words. Minds heighten enabling learning; souls grow ennobling the ones learning. It is in such conditions, the presence of a teacher of such character, that most insights occur—a mutual growth in each one's self-respect. Each one. Had I a chance to speak, I would have read the lines that for me have stood as a dedication. They seem so appropriately fitting to your way:

Few
have the opportunity
to bend history.
But take each one,
each lone person,
here, now.
That's the opportunity
to bend the history of this one,
this one life
whose history is before me.

To teach and love teaching is really to love the students. Your loss of those students, that discourse, dialogue will be felt. Obviously, they will miss you. But whatever you're engaged in, you'll be the same Dan and others will be edified.

I'm glad we'll talk again.
Joe DiIenno

In a number of ways, my retirement dinner was a prelude to the annual district dinner held for the primary purpose of honoring those of us retiring. That dinner was scheduled for June 3, 2005 at Blue Heron Pines in Egg Harbor Township. Prior to the dinner, Dr. Pfeffer reminded me of his assignment: an oral presentation in response to the question, WHAT IS A TEACHER?

Before sharing that presentation, I defer, momentarily, to Tom and Mary Ellen Schurtz who presented me with a photo album created by them for my initial retirement dinner on May 6, 2005. The album is striking as a record of the many faces who attended the affair. It became even more striking upon my examining it to find a section following the photographs which contained the written words that Tom had spoken at my retirement dinner. He praised me as a teacher and supervisor and, like Joe DiIenno, included several significant comments relating to the definition of a teacher. As a master teacher himself and a former teacher of the year at Absegami, Tom offers cogent insights about defining attributes of "teacher."

My grandmother instilled the seed of the idea of teacher in me. Brother Anthony Wallace nurtured that seed. Newark Central High damned near choked it. But Dr. Walters made the dream come true. If I can be called a teacher, it is because of Dr. Walters.

Teaching is an instinctual art, smacking of potential, craving of realizations. It is a pausing, seamless process, where one rehearses constantly while acting. One sits as a spectator at the play that he directs. The work of a teacher—exhausting, complex, idiosyncratic, never the same twice—is at its heart, an intellectual and ethical enterprise. Teaching is the vocation of vocations. It is an activity that is intensely practical and yet transparent. It is brutally matter-of-fact, and yet fundamentally a creative art. It requires leadership based on substance and caring. The extraordinary work that our department has produced only emerges if the teachers are exposed to extraordinary models. Dr. Walters is one of those models.

J.D. Salinger, through his character of Mr. Antollini (a teacher) tells us that educated and scholarly men, if they are brilliant and creative to begin with tend to leave infinitely more valuable lessons behind them. They tend to express themselves more clearly and they have a passion for following their thoughts through to the end. Looks like old JD peaked out of his bombshelter long enough to meet Doc.

I am humbled by Tom Schurtz's inspirational and praiseworthy comments. I am so grateful that he and his wife Mary Ellen included those comments in the photo album. Tom was a model teacher, and his thoughts and those of Joe DiIenno at my retirement dinner would have an impact on the outcome of my response to Dr. Pfeffer's assignment. Before I turn to the fulfillment of that assignment, I must pay final respects to Tom and Mary Ellen Schurtz, both of whom passed away a year and a half apart. Mary Ellen died from cancer on July 17. 2017, and Tom died from a heart attack on January 7, 2019. Ironically, Tom was working as a substitute teacher and preparing for work when he collapsed. Both appear in Chapter 24 of this memoir among my eulogies. Their untimely deaths have left many broken hearts.

30

JUNE 3, 2005...WHAT IS A TEACHER?

Once again I found myself in a sling as Maria drove through another wind-swept rainstorm to Blue Heron Pines in Galloway Township, New Jersey, for the Greater Egg Harbor Regional's Annual District Dinner celebrating retiring staff on June 3, 2005. I received a beautiful plaque which read:

AWARDED TO

Daniel N. Walters, Ed.D.
In Recognition of
Dedicated Service to the Youth of this
School District
1962 to 2005
Board Of Education
Greater Egg Harbor Regional
High School District

Maria and I (in my sling) at Retirement Celebration

Celebration

By the time I retired, we were three schools in the district: Oakcrest (where I began my teaching career), Absegami (where I ended my career), and Cedar Creek, a magnet school, located in Egg Harbor City. I was very proud of my years of service and can truly say that I never had a bad day during my career. I did not retire complaining about my workload; I did not experience what people call **burnout**; I loved my staff; I loved my students; I enjoyed supervising five different departments: English, Reading, Drama, Media and Dance. Forty years as an educator certainly provided me with insights about teachers and the art of teaching. Mr. Schurtz suggested that I was instrumental in his evolution as a teacher. I, in turn, can say that my quality of performance was strengthened by the exceptional talent of a Mr. Schurtz and other teachers like him who helped me evolve.

Let's get back to June 3, 2005. I am ready for my close-up as I am introduced by Dr. Adam Pfeffer and a culminating presentation about a word and world that I have been a part of for over forty years: TEACHER.

WHAT IS A TEACHER?

We all know what a teacher is, just as we know what love is, justice is, or truth is. And, like those elusive qualities which we struggle with to teach the meaning of, TEACHER, too, defies definition much like that defiant

199

adolescent who we might have been or certainly may have confronted in the classroom as he or she attitudinally asked, "What could you possibly teach me?" That student, of course, was thoroughly familiar with Clint Eastwood and those Spaghetti Westerns and Clint's later filmic quip, "Go ahead and make my day!"

And so, the CHALLENGE: TEACHER: Someone who performs the tango, the minuet, tarantella or some other motivational western dance to engage learners—sometimes intractable—in seizing the day and making something of it.

Then, of course, there is the student who knows a good deal when he sees it, and if he doesn't see it, he plots long and hard to make sure that the teacher sees it. That brings to mind another Clint Eastwood in my collection of memorable students in my search for defining TEACHER, my former student, Chuck Breitzman. Now, let me first say that Chuck and I did not get off on the best foot back in 1982. I made a dreadful mistake by calling him Charley. His reaction was quite Clint Eastwood as he let me have it with both barrels and readily straightened my curly hair informing me (and I never forgot it) that his name was CHUCK. Underneath that cowboy hat and boots, I had sensed a rather extraordinary intelligence—not through any of his overt behavior—but certainly through indicators—teachers look for things like that.

And so, the CHALLENGE: TEACHER: Someone who wants to turn Charley around and accepts the challenge of being challenged, breaking through, surveying new ground, sometimes having to make a deal. Well, all of those lofty goals were obviously not Chuck Breitzman's. We were both smart, but he, of course, had the last word—dealing teenagers often do! And so, we made a deal. He would not have to write a traditional term paper if he prepared, delivered, and participated in the annual American Legion's Oratorical Contest focusing on some phase of the Constitution. I still ask myself to this day how we got there after that whole Charley fiasco. But we did. Did we ever! Charley Chuck Breitzman won the Atlantic County Division of that contest and went on to place in the state finals! For the state finals, we even hired a bus and loaded up a bunch of screaming kids making the happy journey from Mays Landing to Trenton to hear Charley Charles Chuck Norman Breitzman deliver his oratory. Did he ever make my day! By the way, can you believe that Chuck Breitzman ended up teaching in my English Department? I am sure it was a plot to haunt and taunt me forever! The day of his victory remains quite a memory for both of us.

It was one day in a long history of extraordinary days in the life of this teacher-supervisor who began teaching at Oakcrest High School in 1962. That search for the meaning of who I was and what a teacher is had begun long before 1962, and the roots for understanding and wanting to be a teacher grew out of my contact and nurturing in the Nesco Grammar School which was renamed after I left; it is now called the Hilda S. Frame School. She was, of course, Mrs. Frame to all four grades that she taught in the same classroom. And what a teacher! In my journey toward becoming a teacher she probably defined it best. When she died on April 17, 1989, I felt a deep sense of loss and shortly thereafter eulogized her in a letter that was published in the Atlantic City Press. Listen to what I had to say about her:

> Teacher she was as she led us to autumn leaves to be pressed, identified, preserved for a lifetime. Lady of tradition she was as she sent me out with one of the bigger kids to chop down our school's tree for the Christmas season. Primavera she was as she led a band of excited students into the woods in search of Trailing Arbutus in the spring of the year. Yes, we loved her, for you see she sparkled and sparked life and interest in learning as only the great teachers know how. There was something about that beautiful voice of hers; it was a musical instrument. With it, she took us down the Mississippi with Tom Sawyer and Huckleberry Finn. With it, she taught us how to spell and articulate. With it, she flashed the silver skates of Hans Brinker and dug up history, both ancient and American. With it, she led us into a world of books, questions and answers, and all of the wonders of the universe.

Hilda S. Frame was, indeed, a teacher ahead of her time as she orchestrated as many as four grades in a single classroom which merged into an "open" learning environment. Open it was—open to a universe of possibilities where eighth graders mingled with fifth graders, where ideas of science, literature and the arts melded together and forged a collection of rich images and never-to-be forgotten firsts in the hallowed halls of our school and our minds. Among those images stands Hilda S. Frame, a teacher's teacher, my most memorable.

Listening to my memories of Mrs. Frame, you may very well have heard me say something that struck you personally; for some of the greatest teachers that have ever lived are sitting in our midst. I have thought, on occasion, how interesting it would be to take the great qualities of the great teachers I have known, put them in a blender, and push the buttons on the old Osterizer Pulse-Matic to blend, shred, grind, frappe, stir, beat, liquefy, chop, whip, and mix to see what the end result might be. Somehow I sense that the essence of that concoction would dissolve into a formula so rich in texture and composition that many of us sitting here would recognize it as a Fineberg, Irene Fineberg,

In my search for a definition of TEACHER and its defining attributes, Mrs. Fineberg must be included. As I told that committee from Princeton: Let me begin by stating that one seldom encounters a teacher like her. She is that remarkable teacher who leaves indelible impressions, impressions as rich as the extraordinary blending of line and color contained in great works of art. She is an artist in the field of education, and the classroom is her studio wherein she deftly works to shape minds and spirits as she ignites imaginations to write creatively or to travel the Rhine and scale the Alps immersed in learning German. I sometimes think of her classroom as a grand piano that is constantly being tuned, for as Mrs. Fineberg processes the content of a lesson (often the students themselves), she periodically steps back to assess the quality of the performance, makes an adjustment and then proceeds through another sequence of the lesson, fine-tuning sounds, clarity of thought, and a myriad of other instrumental structures.

I ended my letter to the Dean of Princeton with the following vignette: I recall one of Mrs. Fineberg's students commenting, "She rocks!" I am sure I looked puzzled, at first, but then understood the profoundness of the student's observation. Mrs. Fineberg does rock; she is heard rocking via the groundbreaking, volcanic classroom eruptions, and through her daily orchestrations and punctuations where minds and spirits soar beyond the four walls of this very gifted teacher and rock around the clock wishing that German class would never end.

This past fall, Chip Garrison's production of Shakespeare's **Twelfth Night** was dedicated to Tom Schurtz, another rocker who is also retiring this year. Mr. Schurtz's legacy is monumental, and in my search for defining TEACHER I would be remiss by not including him. I referred to him once as a Pied Piper watching students follow his lead as he challenged them to look beyond the grade, to take delight in matters of intrinsic worth, urging them to cast their reels into Thoreau's heavens which are pebbly with stars. At the core of this master teacher is an empathy for kids and an ability to engage, to have them reach beyond their grasp as he melds life and literature and Shakespeare into a tapestry of memorable scenes, characters and lessons for life that will live on.

As this phase of my search for the meaning of TEACHER draws to a close, I defer to Anne Cognard, an English supervisor from Lincoln, Nebraska whose enthusiasm for the Bard has brought her international recognition. For her, teaching is more artistry than science, more organic than planned, more serendipitous than mechanical. The interaction between teacher and student is like the growth of an animal or human being. Chance combined with art creates a miraculous result. She builds on that idea of artistry by referencing the well-known director Peter Brook who replied when asked how his plays work, "…one chooses the roles for each actor (the student), the vision (the curriculum), the approach (the pedagogy), and the collegiality one brings oneself (the teacher)." Then, one rehearses (the daily process of learning and taking chances). If it all works, one says, "Ah." For Anne Cognard, that is teaching. The DEFINITION: A TEACHER, someone who brings self, vision, idealism, excitement, knowledge and empathy, chooses the what and how of the curriculum, responds to the quirks of students, and then rehearses, bringing all this together in the daily development of movements in knowledge and understanding—seemingly simple, yet intricately complex.

What a startling phrase, MOVEMENTS IN KNOWLEDGE AND UNDERSTANDING: Chuck Breitzman coming to terms with the Constitution and speaking eloquently; the Little Ones of Irene Fineberg for whom the obstacles of life were turned into lessons of creative problem solving, seeking to unlock what seemed alien or cryptic in literature—what seemed puzzling in life itself, or as in my case, recalling no schooling before the second grade, growing up as a ward of the state, finding the music of language and love of learning from Hilda S. Frame whose incomparable lessons of life echo today through those remarkable movements in knowledge and understanding that make the meaning of teacher so very clear.

And so, to the students and teachers whom I have taught, the colleagues whose respect has allowed me to function and grow, to my magnificent special teacher and mentor, my wife Maria, to a district that I have called home for more than forty years, and to Dr. Pfeffer without whom this search for the definition of TEACHER might never have occurred, I say, THANK YOU.

* *

I conclude this chapter with two additional tributes to teachers from the Absegami English Department. Each further enhances the definition of "teacher." I presented the first piece in 2004, a year before my retirement when Mrs. King retired from the district.

Donna Lewis King

Robert Frost challenged us with "The Road Not Taken"; Donna Lewis King showed him a thing or two by taking not only that road but cutting a few paths of her own! Lucky for us that she made that right-hand turn off the Black Horse Pike and then another right turn landing her smack in the middle of the GEHRSD (Greater Egg Harbor Regional High School

District—the "D" actually stands for DONNA; she would eventually have dominion over all!

Like that haunting melody from the 1950's—a distant generation for some of you sitting out there, although some of you probably wailed the song from your cribs and your carriages: "I Knew A Girl And Donna Was Her Name"-- like all of the great Donnas, Donna King had a way of making a difference whether traveling down Route 66, Route 40, Route 30, Great Creek, Jimmie Leeds, or Wrangleboro Road. All roads lead to someone special, and Donna L. King is without question one special great lady!

Funny, isn't it, how sometimes you are the very essence of your name. DONNA, from the Italian for lady. Once, twice, three times a lady, Lady Donna, but of course that wasn't enough for her; she had to go and marry Kevin King, thereafter dubbed Donna King, making her the only dual ruling Donna in the Absegami-Oakcrest complex: Lady Queen Donna Lewis (that's actually Louie) the King!

I've actually lost count of the number of years I've known her ladyship which is probably a good thing for both of us! What I do remember, and what has been good for all of us, is that Donna Lewis King possesses a singular magic—a Midas touch, if you will, in her ability to teach, to lead out, to help struggling readers see beyond the words and feel the pain of those aboard the Amistad, or empathize with Jane Eyre as a blind Mr. Rochester professes a love deeper than words, or visualize on another road with Robert Frost as he recollects:

> You ought to have seen what I saw on my way to the village
> Through Mortenson's pasture today
> Blueberries as big as the end of your thumb,
> Real Sky-blue, and heavy, and ready to drum
> In the cavernous pail of the first one to come!
> And all ripe together, not some of them green
> And some of them ripe, you ought to have seen
>
> FROST ("Blueberries," Lines 1-7)

And, yes, you ought to have seen the magic I have seen Donna Lewis King weave, transporting young readers to new heights, helping them decipher, decode, and make sense of a world that we often take for granted. How she struggled, at times, with the rudiments to help students see beyond the main idea. In all the years of her teaching, she captured imaginations, built trust, fostered a willingness to learn, and successfully helped children from the farthest reaches of our district and from the far corners of the earth LEARN HOW TO READ!

Well, Mrs. King, I sense that your journey is far from over, and that you have a few more pints of blueberries to pick. I thank you for the road we have traveled. All of us salute you, wishing every happiness in your retirement.

* *

The final teacher tribute is about someone whom you have already met as a central figure in my extended definition of a teacher. Imagine the pride I felt two years after my retirement when I was invited to a Teacher of the Year celebration for none other than Chuck Breitzman. Here is what I had to say:

Chuck Breitzman

A friend of mine uses the expression, "I raised him or her," referring to someone that he helped rear or grow up. I can proudly say that I helped raise CHUCK BREITZMAN, first as his teacher, and later as his supervisor.

Underlying the relationship was always a recognition, on my part, of a young man with extraordinary potential, a genuine love for the written word, a willingness to accept a challenge (and, at times, to challenge), and the ability to teach me or his students a thing or two. Today marks a high point in Mr. Breitzman's career: Teacher of the Year—a deserving accolade for someone whose demonstrated mastery in the art of teaching is a solid reason for pause. I have always loved his sense of humor—even when the kids (and some adults) didn't get it. I also admired his use of technology as a tool for instruction, but I admired even more the larger than life ranting

Mr. Breitzman who thunderously employed vocal and seismic-inducing rumblings and grumblings to keep them awake, to sustain focus, to empha-size a point, or to bore something into thick sculls! "Oh, Mr. Breitzman," they would yell back forcing him to spew lava all over the classroom—what a sight! Not an easy act to follow, Mr. Breitzman.

Lucky students, lucky district, lucky Absegami, lucky all of us for having endured your wrath and volcanic explosions. Lucky are we to have a Chuck Breitzman in our presence.

Mercurial, temperamental, and swashbuckling, Mr. Breitzman is the man of the hour for whom those immutable images on John Keats' Grecian Urn are as powerful today as they were 2500 years ago reflecting the beauty and truth in life, just as Mr. Breitzman reflects the sustaining power and impact of great teachers, past and present, for whom the Grecian Urn and the teaching profession endure, standing as monuments to truth and beauty and what is essential in our lives as we are raised up. Thank you, and congratulations, Mr. Breitzman.

* *

A closing note for this chapter is to the memory of another influential teacher in my life. Ken Frisbee was my foster father's brother-in-law. I met him and Aunt Esther, Father Brown's sister, in the 1950's shortly after my sister Margie, brother Victor, and I were placed with the Browns. I called Ken Frisbee, Uncle Bud, and remember how interested he was in my plan to become a teacher. He was a superintendent of schools in Freehold, New Jersey and urged me to keep in touch with him when I began job hunting. As it turned out, I readily found a teaching position but was grateful for his interest. Maria and I visited Uncle Bud and Aunt Esther when they were living in Brooks, Maine. Years later, they passed away living on a mountain in North Carolina. They were true pioneers. I recall many things about Uncle Bud, but the most significant memory is that he is the first person I remember looking at me and saying, "We love you very much, Danny."

31

STUDENT VOICES FROM THE PAST

In his letter to me following the May 6, 2005 retirement dinner, Joe DiIenno commented, "To teach and love teaching is really to love the students." The impact of that statement is powerful and evokes a sampling of students whom I remember fondly, thinking back to my forty plus years as an educator. I have already cited several memorable students in the pages of this memoir. Here are the names of some others that come to mind: Sandy Pack, George Spivey, Tina Monroe, Arlene Gullo, Sherry Hyde, Wesley Meier, Arthur Spenser, Grace Austin, Bob Hennessey, Janet Imperatore, Anna Wapnik, Bobby Gasko, John Sahl, Susan Heuman, Jason Merkoski, Lucia Woo, Stephen Koval, Jacqueline Kelsch, Michael Ring, Anne Grunow, Jason Herlands, Beverly Whaley, Ingrid Butler, Gary Melton, Jackie Storhaug, Nicholas Petruzzi, Alythea McKinney, Matt Guenther, Doug McCullough, Kathy Schroeder, Robert Bucknam, Mary Lou Broker, Jeff Frack, Sharon Castrenze, Ripal Gandhi, Raymond Gifford, Kathy Johnson, George Fleming, Dana Walters, Jack McCallum, Linda Johnson, Bill Weir, Robert Madeira, Mike Gardner, Don Randall, Isi Jacoby, Barbara Sauerwald, Joey Eichinger, Peter Kubaska, Anne Robson, Linda Spendiff, and all of those Absegami Valedictorians and Salutatorians whom I coached through the years. Within the scope of this memoir, it's impossible to list everyone whom I taught or with whom I had a special connection. Be assured, many students not listed here have, at times, come to mind in moments of reverie. All of them, in some way, lifted my spirits, helped me realize the awesome responsibility I had as a teacher, broadened my perspective about life, and, in a word, were loved.

The voices of several other students from the past have earned a special place in my heart because of their accomplishments or tributes over the years. In a semester course I designed and taught, entitled WHY MAN CREATES, I met a very talented student named Concetta Maria Stoto who went by Katie. At the end of the course, she submitted a journal of her writings and sketches, along with a poem she dedicated to me.

> And from the seed of our days
> Will rise my rich harvest of
> Memories which chose to stay;
> It will tickle and refresh my mind
> As on the wind of time
> It dances and plays—
> And I love you,
> My mentor of a season

Thirty years had passed when Katie Stoto arrived at my office on June 10, 2005 with a special gift for my retirement:

To: <u>Dr. Daniel Walters</u>

> My teacher hovers down the hallway,
> his red curls and music notes
> trailing behind him.
> What he cultivated into my mind
> and fed to my soul intravenously
> has nourished me for thirty years.
> Again we are children
> running behind him,
> chasing a beautiful airborne kite!

Returning to school after my brother Victor died in December 1973 was a bit emotional. Fortunately, I was teaching a nine-week Expository

Writing class to a group of amazing seniors who managed every day to lift my spirits. When the course ended in late January, the students presented me with a booklet of writings entitled ME/WE composed during the class. An independent project, the booklet contained eight writing sections: ME THINKS, OBSERVANCE, NATURE, DEATH, IMAGINATION, FABULOUSLY FUNNY, LOOKING BACK, and LOST AND FOUND. Each section was introduced with a dividing sheet on which were sketched cartoon-like images of me whom they had used as a mascot. The introductory page to the IMAGINATION section featured me wearing a brightly colored floral tie for which the students had employed colored pencils to highlight each of the flowers on the tie. Imagine, they did that for all of the booklets printed. Thinking back, I am intrigued by the parallel between this group of high school seniors and the first graders in the Williamstown Integrated Arts Project where a group of first graders called me Mr. Purple in response to a floral tie I was wearing; one of the students had actually drawn a picture of me with a crayon-colored purple tie.

Now, forty-five years after the creation of that ME/WE collection, I thank a group of students, particularly Mike Gardner, Mark Noll, Ed Pappas, Jeff Frack, Tom Boselli, Don Ross, Maureen Holmes, Sue Blanchard, Kathy Johnston, Pam Wells, and all of the students whose writing comprised the publication. The booklet is a treasure trove independently student-driven to house selected pieces of writing developed during the nine-week writing course.

David Warker's essay, "Our Woods," in Chapter 16 is from the ME/WE collection. I have selected one additional piece from that collection for inclusion in this memoir; the piece is found in the final section of the booklet entitled LOST and FOUND. Written by eighteen year-old Arthur Harper, it is entitled, A LETTER FROM MY MIND.

A LETTER FROM MY MIND

Dear Mr. Walters,

As we near the end of this nine week journey together, there is much I want to say to you. Even now as I write, my mind moves much too fast for my hand to keep up with it. So much has happened in so short a time. Time, it's funny how each of us races against it trying to do what we want to do or have to do in the time given us. Some manage fairly well while others fight a losing battle. Perhaps this is because some are given more time than others.

You, you were given nine weeks, nine short weeks to try to undo what it had taken me eighteen years to build. In eighteen years I had built my own little world apart and separate from everything and everyone around me. It was a world in which emotions and feelings are not to be seen. Oh, I had feelings but I was afraid to let them out for I did not know what to expect. So in my own little world I retreated because it was easier that way, to escape and run away from what I felt. It was a cold world, my world, as cold as an iceberg at times, and many times I wanted to get out, but once you are on an iceberg you are trapped into captivity by a sea of coldness just waiting to drown you; and so, you must wait until a ship passes if you are to escape.

My ship finally came by, and I decided to try my plans of escape. It was hard at first, and it still is at times. I guess it will always be like that, but I have now landed and begun to take root like a yearling tree. I know now that like that tree if I am to grow tall and strong with branches of great beauty and power, I must have roots. I must have deep, long roots, roots that touch and feel the roots around me. I, like that tree, must have these roots to be able to stand in all weathers and challenge the test of time.

It is a slow process, though. I know that and like the tree which reaches for the sun, I may never reach my goal, but I must try for there is only faith now. I still am afraid of my feelings at times but I will be able to overcome that, for like the sting of a cold winter's day in December, it is feeling life and expressing those feelings that make life meaningful.

Arthur Harper

I initially selected Arthur's thoughtful piece of writing for this memoir without knowing what had happened to him after graduation. An internet search again paid off leading me to believe that what Arthur found in that Expository Writing class was a prelude, perhaps, to developing his roots, feeling life and expressing feelings. What I learned from my search about Arthur Harper is astonishing. After graduating from Stevens Institute of Technology with a degree in Chemical Engineering, he went on to become a History Maker and was awarded the Black Achievers in Industry Award in 1994, the Career Achievement Award at Stevens Institute of Technology in 1998, and the Social Justice Award from the Fairfield County Region National Conference for Community and Justice. Further, Arthur oversaw GE Plastics in Europe, the Middle East, India and Africa. In May, 2000, he became President and Senior Managing Director for GE Plastics Europe; he was also President of GE Plastics in Greater China. When Arthur retired from GE, he started his own private equity firm, NexGen Capital Partners.

What amazing accomplishments! Looking back at his words in "A Letter from My Mind,": "I have now landed and begun to take root like a yearling tree.

I know now that like that tree if I am to grow tall and strong with branches of great beauty and power, I must have roots." And, what roots Arthur Harper put down during the forty-four years since I had taught him!

Sadly, Arthur passed away at age sixty-one on September 19, 2017.

* *

-

CHRISTINA M. CRAIGE

What a rich life I have had as a teacher. The pulse and heart of the school were always the students whose voices continue to reverberate, flashbacks reminiscent of Wordsworth's daffodils, recollections in tranquillity. As I shape this chapter about memorable students, one Christina Craige flashes before me, and I begin the search to uncover what direction her life took beyond her graduation from Absegami in 1997. Christina's mother is an avid bridge player, and I was able to get her telephone number from another passionate bridge player, our next door neighbor, Billie Jane Maul. Through one phone call, I retrieved an e-mail address for Christina, now living in Glendale, California. Eureka! I was on the road to capturing the "voice" of an extraordinary young woman with whom I had had no contact for twenty-two years. On May 2, 2019, I sent the following e-mail to Christina:

Dear Christina,

I spoke with your mom today; we had a nice chat. I asked her for a way of contacting you as I am in the throes of writing a memoir. A chapter of my memoir will be devoted to "Student Voices from the Past." My interest is a letter or comment from you looking back to our time together, your accomplishments, etcetera. You decide what you might like to pass on to me as a tribute and/or bio information reflecting your studies and professional work. A copy of your resume would be helpful. I have onlypleasant memories of you as a former, gifted student.

On May 7, 2019, I received the following e-mail from Christina:

Dear Dr. Walters,

So nice to hear from you. When were you hoping to have the final comment/contribution from me? I'm happy to participate and would like to give it some thought, but also want to be cognizant of your timeline and internal deadline. I have attached a recent resume which should give you some insight on what I've been doing since graduation. Most recently, I switched law firms and took on a new position that has afforded me more time to spend with my family. Another thing it has enabled me to do is to read more, at least for pleasure (since so many of my days have been spent reading and writing for work.) After reading a few fluffy fantasy novels (ever my genre of choice), I decided I wanted to tackle the Time Magazine Top 100 Novels (since the magazine's inception—just narrowly missing Ulysses). I majored in English and Latin in college but spent considerably more time on poetry and earlier periods than the 20th. Century. Okay, I suppose I've rambled long enough (I probably could have written your requested insert by now, but do truly want to mull a bit. I have also attached a picture of referenced precocious nearly 6 year old (she would correct that she is 5 and 11/12 if she were reading this, which she could with substantial comprehension).

More soon,
Chris

In a subsequent e-mail dated May 21, 2019, I received the following from Christina:

I first met Dr. Walters in his office—a small space withina larger project area—when I entered Absegami High Schoolas a sophomore. I came from a very religious and rather backward educational environment in which I was told by my 5thgrade teacher that she wanted to teach high school English but didn't think it was appropriate to teach men of a certain age. Absegami was at least twice as large as my prior K-12 school. I met Dr. Walters with my mother, who had brought me prior to the start of school, to determine which level of classes would be appropriate for me. I had always been a "straight A" student.I learned that day that I had failed the entrance exam to Algebra and would be told later by a science teacher that I should consider going back and taking ninth grade science. (In fairness to them, I probably did more sentence diagramming than my peers, even if *Animal Farm* had been off-limits for book reports).Dr. Walters continued to support me throughout my studies at Absegami. In fact, he even traveled to Washington, D.C. in my senior year to see me accept a Scholastic Writing Award for a science fiction story I had written. I found in him a sponsor and a mentor at a time in my life when I needed both. He encouraged a love of English and literature that continues to this day.

Chris

Thinking back to that day in August, 1994, when I first met Carol Craige and her daughter Christina, I recall a bright and articulate young woman anxious to be scheduled into a challenging English program. Our Honors/AP Programs fit the bill, and Christina was off and running. I texted her for some additional information about her Absegami experience, in particular, along with some additional information related to her college training and professional work as an attorney. She cited several formative Absegami experiences, including participation in the Emanon Players (Drama Club), Mock Trial, and the English class with Mr. Thomas Schurtz, a highly positive, influential teacher. Following graduation, she was accepted into the Rutgers College Honors Program where she excelled earning a Bachelor of Arts in English and Latin in 2001. Her senior Henry Rutgers thesis was on Catullus and Sir Thomas Wyatt. The degree was impressive but even more impressive were the additional honors she had earned: *summa cum laude*, Phi Beta Kappa, and valedictorian for Rutgers College. Remember, this was the incoming sophomore at Absegami who failed the Algebra entrance exam and was advised to go back and take ninth grade General Science! In an e-mail exchange, I made a request for a copy of Christina's valedictory address. She responded in a May 30, 2019 e-mail:

Unfortunately, I do not have a copy of my valedictory speech from Rutgers, but I can tell you that it was inspired, and punctuated, by the song "Bookends" by Simon and Garfunkel. I hadn't decided how I would deliver the 6 lines during the course of the speech (I had broken them into 3 couplets, with the first as the beginning of my speech). I decided at the dais that I would sing them. I will always remember the hush of surprise that fell on the quad.

After Rutgers, Christina continued her education at Yale where she acquired a Master of Business Administration and a Juris Doctor degree, both completed between 2002 and 2006. She was a judicial clerk for the District of Connecticut for 2006-2007. From 2007 through 2015 she was a Restructuring Associate for Sidley Austin LLP. In her own words from her Profile:

A restructuring attorney with extensive experience in complex transactions and high stakes litigation. I regularly tackle legal issues outside my core area of expertise and focus on delivering practical, business driven advice and solutions. In my roles leading human resources-related committees at Sidley, as well as developing associates and paralegals in my group, I promote a team-oriented, inclusive approach that fosters buy-in and encourages innovative thinking.

At Sidley, Christina was recognized in the spring of 2018 among a listing of People Who Make A Difference. As a restructuring attorney (be it associate, partner, or counsel), Christina guided companies in financial distress, navigating them through their in-court (ie., formal bankruptcy proceedings) or out-of-court options, representing them in court when needed.

Christina's most recent move was to Latham and Watkins LLP where she began her work as counsel. Her experience base with that firm reads as follows:

Specializes in advising boards of directors and senior management in navigating financial and operational restructurings leading to in-court and out-of-court solutions. Extensive experience in structuring, negotiating and drafting complex deal documents and significant legal pleadings, as well as appearing in court. Regularly supervises teams of associates and coordinates with colleagues in other practices (e.g., litigation, employment law, and M&A (mergers and acquisitions) to provide comprehensive and seamless solutions.

What a remarkable young woman! In my mind's eye I can hear Christina's voice while standing at the podium delivering her valedictory address in 2001 at Rutgers College, singing Simon and Garfunkle's lyrics from "Bookends."

Finding Christina after twenty-two years, I stand in awe of her accomplishments. Hers is an eloquent "student voice from the past" evoking within me images of bygone days and the urgency to preserve special memories, realizing they are all that's left.

The voices of Absegami's Arthur Harper and Christina Craige are joined by Oakcrest graduate, Jim Schroeder, whom I taught, along with his children Kathy and James, Jr. His voice appeared in the Opinion Section of *The Current*, a weekly newspaper. Jim was the Atlantic County Freeholder at the time he wrote this.

WALTERS WAS ONE OF OUR GREATEST TEACHERS
Wednesday, September 29, 2010

Thank you for the wonderful article by Suzanne Marino in last week's edition about Dr. Dan Walters and his award-winning entry in the *Old Farmer's Almanac* Essay Contest. Despite growing up in difficult circumstances, Dan Walters worked hard to lift himself up to become one of this areas most outstanding educators. I first met Dan working on a blueberry farm in Nesco (Mullica Township) in the late 1950's. Several years later, I had the good fortune to have Dan as my homeroom and Senior English teacher at Oakcrest High School. While there are many great educators in our schools, Dan had a rare and exceptional capacity to reach his students. He was an inspiration to me, personally, and to hundreds (if not thousands) of the young people he taught at Oakcrest and Absegami High Schools. In his winning essay entry, Dr. Walters cites the impact on his life of a stranger's "simple act of caring." His students will surely attest that it was his intelligence and caring that made him one of the greatest teachers this area has ever seen.

Jim's tribute was a special voice echoing what for me had been a splendid career. My actual retirement date was July 1, 2005, and I vividly recall two of my closest friends, Barbara Noll and Bob Quinn, walking me to my car, a subtle way of saying good-bye.

Little did I know that I would be back at Absegami again the following spring for a most unusual unveiling. That unveiling had a direct connection with the focus of this chapter. The following newspaper article recounts what occurred for me on April 24, 2006: ABSEGAMI HONORARY WALL DEDICATION_

> Dr. Dan Walters, who retired from the Greater Egg Harbor Regional High School District last July, 2005, was recently honored at Absegami High School. For his years of extraordinary service and dedication to the district and students, a Wall of Honor was dedicated to him. The wall, lining a main corridor, contains honorary plaques for all of Absegami's valedictorians and salutatorians from 1972 through 2005, all of whom Dr. Walters coached for their graduation oratories. On April 24, 2006, Dr. Walters joined that gallery of scholastic honorees when Mr. Raymond Dolton, principal, unveiled the wall revealing a dedicatory plaque and a painted script reading:

"In Honor Of Dr. Daniel N. Walters"

Dr. Walters began his career as an English teacher in the district in 1962 and concluded as a supervisor of English, Reading, Drama, Media and Dance. His undergraduate work was done at Glassboro State College, and his Master's and Doctorate were earned at the University of Massachusetts in Amherst. Dr. Walters was the recipient of numerous outstanding educational and departmental citations for his accomplishments throughout his career.

One final note aptly concludes this chapter. The hand-painted script dedicating the wall in my honor was painted by Joel Denmead, a former student whose father's vision so many years ago led to the creation of the Greater Egg Harbor Regional High School District where I spent the larger part of my professional career. Joel's artistic voice in scripting the wall honoring me joins all of those other "Student Voices From the Past" echoing decades of special connections and memories.

(32)

HEART OF ITALY

I began this chapter on June 20, 2019 which marked Maria's and my fifty-fifth wedding anniversary. She is and has been my anchor for all of those years. You have met her family within this memoir, family who, through marriage, became a mother-in-law, brother-in-law, aunts, uncles and cousins to me. When you add that family to the family that has evolved from the Browns, my foster parents, and their relatives, my brother Victor's children, and my sister Margie's daughter and children, I realize how many miles I have traveled since that train ride seventy some years ago from Baltimore to Atlantic City. Rekindled is that moment on the train when the porter gave me a packet of peanut butter crackers which I unwrapped and held the orange colored cellophane to the light seeing a change in perspective, not knowing what the future held for me or my siblings.

I've learned how precious life is and treasure the twenty-thousand and seventy-days that Maria and I have been married as we continue counting the years. On June 20, 2009, I celebrated her in a special poem for our forty-fifth wedding anniversary:

A TOAST TO LOVE

In praise of marriage I joyously sing
 Sixteen thousand four hundred twenty-five
Days spent loving my bride of forty-five

YEARS
Two score plus five who knew we'd survive?

To love, to cherish, in sickness and health
We vowed before God and our family
Echoing promises of brides and grooms
In our march from here to eternity

Come celebrate the joy of blissful marriage
Invoke the Muses led by Terpsichore
Dancing and singing in triumphant glee
Toasting and boasting my long-standing bride

Sixteen thousand four hundred twenty-five
Days, two score plus five, my dear Maria, I love you!

Before we met back in 1963, I recall singing "Maria" from **West Side Story** and playing it on the piano. Little did I know that I would marry a Maria. Our chance meeting at a production of **The Fantasticks** in the summer of 1963 set the stage for our 1964 wedding leading to her accepting the name WALTERS to be added to that beautiful, musical name of hers: Maria Victoria Anna DiGiovanni.

In truth, my last name and hers might have been DONNELLY which we found out fairly recently was my blood father's real last name; he took the name Walters upon moving into a family of Walters. At least, DONNELLY has a cadence to it that would have complimented Maria Victoria Anna DiGiovanni! Well, we have lived with our name this long, and Maria Walters has managed to keep the music playing for fifty-five years.

There are a few more things that I need to tell you about Maria Victoria. She was an English teacher for several years when we taught together at Oakcrest High School back in the 1960's. I already mentioned that we had a yearbook dedicated to the two of us from Sigma, Oakcrest's Class of 1967. We directed the Oakcrest Drama Club together overseeing play direction, wardrobe, make-up, lighting, set design, choreography, program and a host of production-related tasks. During graduate studies at the

University of Massachusetts, Maria was a primary bread winner, working as a clerk typist at the university. She also took courses, earning a Master of Education Degree in Educational Administration.

Following our three years of graduate study at the University of Massachusetts in Amherst, we returned to New Jersey. For a short time, Maria functioned as a school librarian, filling in for someone who was on leave. After that stint, she joined together with her mother Jennie whose linen and handkerchief business, Giovanni's, had been an institution on the Atlantic City Boardwalk since 1927. Maria and her mother Jennie became partners in the business and with the advent of casino gambling, they pursued other locations which led to Central Square in Linwood, New Jersey, an offshore community where Giovanni's thrived and where Maria, at one point, set up M. Walters, a separate very successful bed and bath business.

Mother Jennie passed away in 1985, and Maria assumed control of Giovanni's, demonstrating enormous skill in business acumen and product expansion. Two additional moves occurred over the next fifteen years. Giovanni's moved to Margate City as a small linen boutique, and after several years transitioned to an internet business selling only men's and ladies handkerchiefs, still in operation as I write this memoir.

Having assisted as a salesperson with Giovanni's for a number of years, I became familiar with its dynamics and, particularly, with Maria's role and special qualities that kept the business humming. Elegance is the trademark of Giovanni's, and it is that quality that set the tone for a business that prides itself in catering as a specialty store to a public that recognizes how special it is. As a textile specialist, Maria's refined knowledge, skills and taste are widely recognized. To observe her at work is fascinating as she engages clients in an exchange about fabrics and thread counts that is truly a learning experience. Her interest has always been not only to make a sale but also to cultivate and satisfy the needs and tastes of her customers, some of whom are descendants of the generations of Giovanni's customers served over the past ninety years. Over the years, tablecloths, handkerchiefs and other linens of exceptional quality and value have been the primary staples of Giovanni's, and customers have come to depend on the service, judgment, honesty and presence of Maria DiGiovanni Walters. In many ways, her chief contribution to the business world is her subtle sharing and cultivating of taste and knowledge of textiles.

As a respected member and leader of the Margate Business Association, she has worked to help shape the association's goals for providing services to both businesses and to the larger community. As a member of the Margate Fall Funfest Board of Directors, she was a major voice and innovator in the design and implementation of an extraordinary event, the Margate Fall Funfest, that continues to this day. Working as both a volunteer and implementer of ideas for the Margate Fall Funfest, she planned and chaired key committees, including a juried craft show and a decorating committee which transformed the Margate City bay area into a joyous festival celebrating delicious foods, the arts, the joy of living, and the importance of community. Recognizing Maria's business and civic contributions, the Margate Board of Commissioners awarded her a special proclamation. She was later recognized as one of three business women honored by the Margate Business Association for outstanding service, business acumen, and overall extraordinary contributions as a business owner and leader in Margate's business community.

What a woman! Lucky me to be her husband, and thrilling for the two of us when the Margate Business Association honored us by naming its annual scholarship program, the Daniel and Maria Walters Scholarship which has provided over $105,000.00 in scholarships to Margate students since 1999.

In 2012, Maria celebrated a special birthday for which I put together a surprise birthday party held at Steve and Cookies By the Bay in Margate. It was a memorable evening during which I shared a birthday wish that I had composed:

HAPPY BIRTHDAY, MARIA

Happy birthday, Maria!
What would the world be without you?

Without your Capricorn practicality,
Without your focus and sense of reality
And your sparkling perspicacity?
What would the world be without you
And the friends you have made?
Looking through the calendar year:

January's cold needed warmth and so you were born.

February needed a real heart and you filled the need.

March winds promised winter's end and the return of
spring and you, forever younger than springtime.

April rained umbrella showers but you oft' turned
cloudy days to sunshine and May flowers.

June came busting out all over and you married your
sweetheart the day after his birthday, the same month
as your mother Jennie's birthday.

Summer fun came with July and August and you grew up
in what was truly America's Playground, taking your
first steps on the Boardwalk, growing up in a linen shop,
Giovanni's, selling linens with Jennie and her sisters and
Cousin Marianna, and later creating M. Walters at
Central Square. You've worked your entire life.

September memories recall schooling: St. Michael's, Holy
Spirit, and Cabrini, and teaching at Oakcrest. It was also
the month of Margate's Fall Funfest which you helped to create along with Joe Tozzi and community volunteers.

September 2006 launched a journey that changed your
life forever!

<u>October</u>: That exhilarating month of mists and color, a special month--your brother Paul's and cousin Sister Theresa's birthdays.The search for the perfect pumpkin!

<u>November</u>: Christmas marts and lacing the mincemeat with good Old Jack Daniels Sour Mash and stuffing the turkey with Mario Bongiovanni's Italian sausage and special herbs, making your own cranberry sauce, Thanksgiving delicious!

<u>December</u>: The Fantasticks…Deep in December it's nice to remember Paul and Jennie, and making cioffe with Aunt Millie. Celebrating Joe Tozzi's, Marianna's, and Margie's birthdays, our Christmas tree and beautiful Christmases.

And so, months turn to years, and I ask, "How do you keep the music playing, Maria?" Through your smile, sense of humor, compassion, zest for life, work ethic, special relationships, serving as a sounding board giving support, advice, direction, empathy and love to those who have come to celebrate you. Just one last important ingredient that keeps me singing is your delicious home-made tomato sauce and those awesome Sunday Gravy Dinners: Pasta! Pasta! Pasta!

That's how you keep the music playing, Maria,
HAPPY BIRTHDAY!

Maria Victoria Anna DiGiovanni Walters

In October, 2005, six months after I had broken my shoulder, and three months after my retirement, Maria suffered a heart attack and was rushed by ambulance to the Atlantic City Medical Center. It was a frightening moment. I vividly recall her being transferred to the Mainland Division of the Atlantic City Hospital and found myself running behind a gurney as she was rushed into surgery.

From that gurney she told someone to see that I had something to eat. How Italian! It turned out that Geoff Rosenberger, a close friend, ate my sandwich as I was much too upset to eat. The surgery went well, and Maria told me afterwards how cold it was in the operating room where she remembers praying a Hail Mary, along with a nurse, and singing "God Bless America" as Dr. Howard Levite saved her life by inserting a stent at the back of her heart. Her praise for Dr. Levite continues to this day as she often makes reference to being wheeled into the surgery room, looking up, and intuitively knowing that she was in the hands of a PRO, and she told him so!

Her recovery was remarkable, and although quite weak for a period of time, she recuperated quickly. Following a week's stay in the hospital, she was released, and when she asked me if I had been eating, I told her that I was and that I had eaten the spinach and beans dinner that she was preparing the night she was rushed to the hospital. Upon her release, shortly after I picked her up in the car, she looked at me and said, "Remember that trip we talked about? It's time!"

And so, we immediately began making plans for a trip to Italy that Maria had thought about for years. Her healing time was essential, and she let her doctor know about the planned trip. He, in turn, monitored her progress and gave her a clearance to travel in September, 2006, roughly a year after her surgery. We were very excited about the trip and worked closely for several months with a dear friend and travel agent, Louise Franklin. We purchased a variety of travel books, an audio program for learning Italian phrases and words, and used the internet as a research tool for information, specifically related to the town and region we were planning to visit.

Maria's cousin Sister Theresa Kelly, MFA, who is fluent in Italian, was a key player in helping us to make contacts and follow-up translations for letters from Italy, prior to our September 28, 2006 flight via Alitalia. Louise Franklin, our travel agent, had attempted to make contact with someone about our planned visit to the little town where Maria's father was born; however, she was not successful. Maria had her own plan for making contact with the little village in the Molese Region where her father had lived as a boy, and that plan and the rest of the remarkable narrative about Maria's search for relatives and the town of Macchia DiIsernia can be found in an essay that I completed in 2012, six years after our journey. I entitled it HEART OF ITALY.

Maria's cousin, Sister Theresa Kelly, whose fluency in Italian bridged communication between Maria and her relatives in Macchia D'Isernia, Italy.

HEART OF ITALY

Forty-eight years of marriage to the same woman is something to brag about. If you knew Maria, you'd understand what makes our marriage so special. Her Italian heritage is certainly a plus, for her tomato sauce and other specialties could easily trump any of the Iron Chefs on Food Network. Our journey together has had memorable peaks and valleys. Let me share one of those unforgettable turn of events that was realized following her heart attack in 2005.

I never knew Maria's father, Paolo DiGiovanni; he died when she was a junior in high school. Through the course of our married life, an oval framed photograph of him and stories about his 1913 journey from Macchia D'Isernia to America kept him alive. He and his brother Loreto settled in Atlantic City, New Jersey where Paolo married Jennie Martino and fathered two children, Paul, Jr. and Maria Victoria, my wife. Jennie died in 1985, and Paul, Jr. in 1990. With their passing and Maria's unexpected heart attack in 2005 came a realization: she was the last living DiGiovanni in her immediate family. That realization set the stage for a remarkable journey as she commented, "Remember that trip we talked about? It's time." That trip would transport us to her father's beloved birthplace in the Molese Region of Italy, the little town of Macchia D'Isernia.

Preparing for the trip and not knowing if any immediate relatives were living, we took a chance and researched the Internet. Luckily, Maria located an on-line Italian directory for Macchia D'Isernia which listed addresses for nine DiGiovannis. With assistance, we composed a letter in Italian explaining who we were and our plan to visit on September 28, 2006 in search of records or relatives of Paolo DiGiovanni who had emigrated from Macchia to America in 1913 and returned only once in 1930. We mailed the letters to all nine DiGiovannis in mid-August.

Surprisingly, just two weeks before our flight a letter arrived from Italy. Back to the computer for a startling revelation in the translation of the letter postmarked September 6, 2006:

Your letter was given to me by one of the DiGiovannis
living in Macchia D'Isernia. I read it and realize that we
are your closest relatives. I am Mario Daziani, the son of
Natalina DiGiovanni who was the sister of Loreto and Paolo,
the children of Pasquale and Vittoria DiGiovanni. I hope I
have explained myself well. I leave you with a fond embrace
and hope to see you soon!

Mario

Within twenty-four hours an e-mail arrived:

Dear Cousin Maria Vittoria, I am Filomena, the daughter of
Pacilia DiGiovanni, sister of Natalina, Paolo, Loreto, Esterina,
and Assunta. For years we have tried to find descendants of
Paolo and Loreto. Dear cousin, it would make me very happy
if when you arrive on September 28th you could spend the
day with us. We wait for you with great affection. Ciao—see
you soon!

Filomena

Overwhelmed by the news and anticipation of meeting new-found
relatives, we finalized plans and flew Alitalia from Newark to Rome on
September 25th. Three days later, with a bouquet of flowers in hand, Maria,
Joe Tozzi, a long-time friend, and I boarded a regional train for Isernia
where we met Barbara Avicioli, a gifted interpreter, who had been requested
through our travel agent to spend the day with us; and, Giovanni Stasi,
Filomena's son, who was waiting at the train station to greet us. Following
introductions, we climbed into Barbara's van and followed Giovanni down
the "yellow brick road" for four kilometers through climbing hills to
Macchia D'Isernia's town square where a gathering awaited.

As we stepped from the van, there was silence. Maria thought she
might have offended someone by wearing slacks. Relying on Barbara, our
interpreter, she learned that the crowd was reacting to how young she was.
Oh happy day as Maria reached out with tears to her new family, embrac-
ing first cousin Mario and his wife Palmina, followed by a whirlwind of

introductions before we left for Mario's house where we shared finger food and photographs brought from America. Family pictures excited interest as we observed a strong resemblance between Grandfather DiGiovanni and Maria's brother Paul. Suddenly someone shouted "Esterina!" and went to find her picture which closely resembled Maria's godmother, Victoria Formica. Drawn to a photograph on the wall of Maria's father and his brother, we learned that Mario's mother Natalina had hung it there the day the two brothers left for America in 1913; it has hung there ever since.

From Mario's we cobblestoned to meet first cousins Filomena and Pasquale. Overcome with emotion, Filomena greeted us with hugs, kisses and tears as we gave her the bouquet purchased in Rome. After more introductions we sat down to a sumptuous home-made meal toasting one another and feasting on a banquet of courses. Throughout the meal our interpreter laughed and cried with us as she brilliantly bridged our two worlds. At one point, Palmina asked Maria how old she was, and then, "How old was your father when he made you?" Everyone applauded when Maria told them he was forty-six. Shortly after, a poignant moment occurred when a cousin shared the story of her wedding dress for which Maria's father had mailed the fabric from America over fifty years ago. After dinner, cousin Pasquale, who told us he was eight years old when Maria's father visited in 1930, took us for a walk. His limited English included the phrase, "Come on." Approaching Maria's father's house, I could feel her heartbeat as she paused to bow her head, reaching out to touch the door. We passed signoras sitting high above us on tiny balconies, "Buona sera." A clearing offered a panoramic view of picturesque beauty. Looking into the valley, Maria asked cousin Mario how her father could have ever left. He explained that although the DiGiovanni family was the second wealthiest in the town, it wasn't enough. Paolo and Loreto had left to strike it rich in America. "Come on," Pasquale beckoned us to the village church where we prayed and then toured Macchia's historic castle. Back in the village piazza we were greeted by the mayor who read aloud a special proclamation honoring Maria's visit.

Our journey almost over, Maria asked to visit the family cemetery where we saw tombstones with small oval pictures of the family she had traveled four thousand miles to meet: her grandparents, Pasquale and Vittoria DiGiovanni, and their children, her aunts, Natalina, Esterina, Pacilia, and Assunta. With daylight fading, we returned to our newly found living relatives who had gathered for a last good-by. Although we traveled throughout Italy, the highlight was that day spent in Macchia D'Isernia where the very heart of Italy came to life. Locating first cousins opened the door to a familial connection that has changed our lives forever. And to think that our journey might never have happened had it not been for Maria's heart attack, the Internet, or those nine letters mailed to a distant Italian village. Proud we are to have walked in her father's footsteps and to have embraced his family and a world of simple pleasures. Viva La Famiglia!

(33)

JOURNEY'S END

Because of that remarkable journey to Italy, Maria fulfilled a life-long dream of seeing the village and house where her father had spent his youth. As a result of that unforgettable trip, we now have family that we would never have known. In addition to those five first cousins discovered in Italy with whom we continue to be in touch, Maria also learned that she has cousins in Australia and Switzerland as well as right here in America. Shortly after our return trip from Italy, we received an unexpected phone call from Pasquale Palumbo, living roughly 125 miles from Margate in the town of Nutley, New Jersey, with his wife Gale. It turned out that Pasquale is a second cousin whose grandmother was Esterina, a sister to Maria's father Paolo. We have visited with the Palumbos and our families have bonded.

Writing this memoir has been a truly cathartic experience for me. Looking back over the years and the evolution of the manuscript, along with sifting through and selecting collected writings that appear throughout the memoir, I defer, momentarily, to a question that Maria asked when I was in the midst of writing: "Is there a core idea, theme or message central to what you are writing?" I've thought a lot about her question, and although my hope is for the reader to answer the question independently, I will use the final pages of this closing chapter to provide some insight.

Family—not only is it at the heart of Maria's journey but also at the center of my personal journey as I found myself early on in my life reaching out in search of a home, a mother and a father, after being abandoned. Ironically, my blood mother Madeline died in 1993, the same year that my foster mother, Dorothy Brown, died. I never saw Madeline again after I had traveled to Baltimore for my grandmother Violet Ireland's funeral. My last image of her was as I stood at my grandmother's casket. Although I had hoped as a little boy that my mother would return after leaving us with our father on a street corner outside the train station in Atlantic City, I never fully got over it, especially since I lived with one family who wrote notes saying that my mother would be coming to see me. She never did.

I suppose there will always be a question in my mind as to why she walked out of our lives. This memoir did not answer that question. My hope is for anyone reading this to feel my hurt at being abandoned as a child but not to use it as a crutch. I never did. Better to set one's sights on nature's beauty, the heavens, the stars, and the planets. Rise above life's pings and arrows with the strength, vision and courage of a Maya Angelou.

There is a bright side to all of this, and I can say that for the most part my optimism has been a salvation throughout the years. There are realizations within my memoir, stated or implied, that reinforce its purpose and reasons for convincing me that I had to write it. Let me share some of those realizations:

I will be grateful, always, for the welfare and foster care systems that were instrumental in bringing some stability to our lives even though at one point as I tried to retrieve information about my past, I was told there were no records.

I value the lessons learned through the public school system and the amazing education that I received even though I recall no schooling before the second grade. For the dedicated teachers I have known who instructed me, and for those with whom I taught in public education, I know that the enterprise is a worthy one.

Worthy, too, are the great books that I have read and taught which are avenues to life's inexhaustible plots, themes, characters, and narratives punctuating Thomas Carlyle's quotation, "Literature is the thought of thinking souls."

Through my journey, I learned that someone doesn't have to be a real parent or blood relative to love you or make you feel loved. My Aunt Hazel Landy brought me a little turtle in a dish from Philadelphia, and she periodically sent me a five dollar bill when I attended Glassboro State College. Her mother, Grandmother Craig, saved all of those articles from the newspaper about my accomplishments and gave them to me one day when I was grown up. And, my favorite Uncle Leo, Aunt Hazel's husband, taught me a lot about nature and called me Shakespeare when we were working in the meadows. My hope is for the reader to see and hear through my words and eyes the beauty of nature found in swaying cattails in the marshes, red-winged blackbirds in flight, and the haunting call of the whippor-will on warm summer nights. Besides Aunt Hazel, Uncle Leo and Grandmother Craig, my foster parents, Dorothy and Bill Brown, although not overly affectionate, loved us children as their own. Likewise, the family that I inherited upon marrying into the DiGiovanni family truly made me feel accepted and loved. My heart is broken as I think back to the many familial exchanges experienced over the years with all of those loving mothers, aunts and uncles who are now deceased, most of whom were not blood relatives.

Like that stranger whom I wrote about for the **Old Farmer's Almanac**, there are other acquaintances whose encouragement and sensitivity deserve recognition, like Camille Young, the attendance secretary at Absegami High School, who walked me to my car the day that I received word at school that Mother Brown had died. Similarly, I will always remember Absegami's Principal, Lynne Basner Gale, taking the time to travel to the little town of Nesco to attend Mother Brown's funeral at the Old Union Hotel. There were others there from school. In particular, I recall one of my departmental teachers, Lori Ranck, years after the funeral, quoting the opening lines of the eulogy I gave at my mother's funeral. Hardly a stranger, another departmental teacher who retired before I did, Terry Much, a good friend and confidante always with the question, "What can I do for you?" Terry was a teacher who heard a different drummer which caught the attention of hundreds of students who still ask about him. In Mr. Much's words, "That's evaluation." And finally, an amazing teacher hardly bound to a wheelchair, Dr. Rosemary Biggio is in the midst of completing a novel as I write this memoir. Her delightful book, ***Crockpot Cooking, A Collection of Prose and Poetry***, published in 2015, was an impetus for me to keep writing.

My abiding interest in the arts was certainly enriched through my graduate studies at the University of Massachusetts. Returning to Absegami High School, I discovered someone with a true passion for her work in the classroom, Maureen Sullivan. What joy she brought to her art students as they painted and sculpted and experimented with varied techniques. How thrilled I was as a teacher to be able to apply ideas from my graduate work by having students interact with Mrs. Sullivan and create works of art linked to literature study. How enduring are the memories of Mrs. Sullivan's end-of-the-year classroom exhibitions of her students' art works. At the end of my career, a young Japanese exchange student from Mrs. Sullivan's class presented me with a beautiful painting she had created employing pointillism.

Also in the realm of the arts are memories of pianist Olga Buttle's golden hands accompanying Maria's brother Paul at the Gateway Playhouse, at our drama productions at Oakcrest High School, and at our wedding in 1964. Always to be remembered, also, was the day Mother Brown played the song "Some Day" on the piano leading to my discovery that I could play the piano by ear. My dear Maria capped that off on my sixtieth birthday by presenting me with a keyboard on which I play music almost every day! Let the music play on!

Yes, there she is once again influencing and shaping my life, Maria Victoria Anna DiGiovanni, the very heart of Italy and the very love of my life. I need to say that a great lesson realized through writing my memoir is that if a man marries the right woman, all is right with the world! We count our blessings every day. My search for a family, begun so many years ago, has mushroomed beyond our imaginations and expectations from one coast of America to the other, to several countries in Europe, and Down Under in Australia.

Through my foster parents and others who influenced my growing up, learning right from wrong, and establishing a set of values to live by, I will always be grateful. In that vain, you may remember from early in this memoir where I wrote about incidents when I was literally trained as a young boy to steal. First, it was a baby carriage from a lobby somewhere in Atlantic City. Later, in another setting, I was coached to steal items from a store using a bag of some kind. Fortunately, one day as I was continuing down that road to damnation as a thief, I found myself reaching to filch a fifty cent piece sitting on a counter at a carnival when a large hand came down to intercede; that hand was big and mighty effective! That hand prevented me from becoming a member of Fagin's Gang!

My closing realization takes me back to the beginning. It is the realization that the impact of great teachers bolsters hope for children like me whose needs were more than learning the ABC's. Hilda S. Frame will always be a star set apart as I recall her orchestrating a universe of possibilities for four different grade levels in a two-room school, in a single classroom, in the little town of Nesco, in the Pine Barrens of Southern New Jersey where this memoir had its very beginnings.